OUT FOR BLOOD

Tales of Mystery and Suspense by Women

VICTORIA A. BROWNWORTH, EDITOR

Third Side Press

Chicago

Printed on recycled, acid-free paper in the United States of America.
Design and production by Midge Stocker.

Acknowledgment
"Jessie" by Katherine V. Forrest originally appeared in *Dreams and
Swords* (The Naiad Press, Inc., 1987). Reprinted by permission of the
author.

Back cover photo credits
Barbara Wilson by Timo Pylvanainen Pressfoto
Ellen S. Korr by Carol Klingensmith
G.V. Babish by JM Redding
J. D. Shaw by JM Redding
Jewelle Gomez by Val Wilmer
Joanne Dahme by JM Redding
Kanani L. Kauka by Jim Marks © 1994
Katherine V. Forret by Maureen Kelly
Kathleen Downey by JM Redding
Lisa D. Willamson by John H. Williamson, Jr.
Mabel Maney by Dina Wilson
Meredith Suzanne Baird by Keryn Lane © 1994
Nikki Baker by D. Scott O'Brien
Ruthann Robson by S.E. Valentine © 1993
Tee A. Corinne by Bev Brown
Victoria Brownworth by Tee A. Corinne

Library of Congress Cataloging-in-Publication Data
Out for blood : tales of mystery and suspense by women / Victoria A.
   Brownworth, editor. - - 1st ed.
      p. cm.
   ISBN 1-879427-20-6 :
   1. Detective and mystery stories, American- -Women authors.
I. Brownworth, Victoria A.
PS648.D4093 1995   94-32350
813'.0872089287- -dc20   CIP

Third Side Press, 2250 W. Farragut, Chicago, IL 60625-1802

First edition, May 1995
10 9 8 7 6 5 4 3 2 1

FOR JMR, WITH DEEP AFFECTION

CONTENTS

Acknowledgments

Anthologies are incredibly hard work; it's almost easier to write a book yourself than to compile the work of other writers. As a consequence, no anthology is the singular work of the editor, much as we editors might like to claim otherwise. I'd like to thank Judith M. Redding, who did a lot of the scut work in the last stages of this anthology—mailing out changes to authors, proofreading seemingly endless revisions of stories after I had, politely nudging late authors when I felt like screaming because of missed deadlines. When my lack of organization threatened to take over, she took charge of coordinating all the tedious bits and pieces essential to the finished manuscript. She was a tremendous help. Ruthann Robson provided a sympathetic ear when I was overly stressed. Tee Corinne, who has edited more anthologies than anyone I know, offered useful suggestions that helped make this a better collection. J.D. Shaw and Lisa Williamson provided last-minute typing assistance. I'd also like to thank Midge Stocker, who is an unabashed feminist in an era when the "f" word is too often considered an embarrassment. Her commitment to publishing the work of women writers is both admirable and essential to our continued struggle for equality. I am happy that she decided to take a chance on genre fiction with this project. Last, but certainly not least, I want to thank all the women who contributed to this anthology, those whose work I used and those whose work I did not.

INTRODUCTION

Victoria A. Brownworth

I have always, since I was a young child, loved mysteries—suspense, detective stories, ghost tales. The first mystery I ever read was *The Ghost of Blackwood Hall* by Carolyn Keene; at eight, it was my introduction to Nancy Drew and my life-long romance with mystery. Carolyn Keene was followed by a host of gothic, mystery, detective, and suspense writers—Agatha Christie, Mary Roberts Rhinehart, Victoria Holt, Phyllis Whitney, Dorothy Eden, Daphne du Maurier, Helen MacInnes, Dorothy L. Sayers were among my favorites. Not surprisingly my first fiction writing as a child was also mystery stories—short tales of detection, the macabre, and international intrigue—which mirrored the work of the women writers of whom I was so fond.

Mysteries are addicting; it's impossible to read just one. I read hundreds of these books as a child, so many that my mother (who had given me my first Nancy Drew) tried to redirect my literary tastes, telling me these books were "trash," insisting that I concentrate on the classics. I often had to sneak my latest favorites out of the library, keeping them hidden from my mother's watchful (and censorial) eye, reading under the covers at night by flashlight. But once I was old enough to read what I chose without adult interference, I always found time for mysteries in addition to my more serious reading. And now, despite my role as literary critic and literature instructor, the books I most *want* to read are still mysteries.

The reason for this, I think, is that my mother's assessment so many years ago was incorrect: These books are *not* (by and large) trash. In fact, just as the most important fiction ever written—those classics my mother was pushing, by Charles Dickens, Jane Austen, George Eliot, Tolstoy, Dostoevsky—falls under the much-maligned category of romance, some mystery fiction is essential to the literary landscape. Some writers of classics, among them Louisa May Alcott and Emily Bronte, are also writers of mystery fiction. And perhaps the most classic (and famous) piece of mystery fiction, *Frankenstein*, was written by a 19-year-old woman, Mary Shelley, whose mother wrote the groundbreaking treatise on feminism, *Vindication of the Rights of Women*. Writers like Georges Simenon, P.D. James, Ruth Rendell, Dashiell Hammett, Dorothy L. Sayers, and Raymond Chandler do more than tell a good story—they reinterpret language and reinvent literary style. And like the authors of the most serious and classic fiction, they examine the most essential aspects of life and challenge the reader's perception of the world.

I have taught college classes in mystery writing for over ten years. I tell my students that mystery writing isn't just the route to a fast buck, although about ten percent of all books published are mysteries and a few writers, like Stephen King, have become millionaires. In addition to teaching them the history of the genre and the basics of the various styles from police procedurals to tales of the supernatural, I also explain how—more than any other books—mysteries are a *necessary* fictional style.

Mysteries are necessary because they allow us to experience all our deepest feelings—especially the murderous ones—without breaking the law. Mysteries also allow us to experience what we so rarely enjoy in our daily lives, a true sense of justice and order. In mystery fiction, evil is always addressed, and not always with the simplicity of a prison sentence. Good usually triumphs in mysteries, though not necessarily in a grandiose—or insipid—manner.

Mystery fiction is also the truest form of modern writing. The characters are caught in the most dramatic and problematic aspects of modern life; mystery protagonists are the quintessentially alienated. Mystery fiction is also, to a certain extent, the one genre where women can—and do—excel without being forced to write with constraints not applied to male writers. In fact, some of the most revered mystery writers, past and present, are women, including Agatha Christie, P.D. James, Ruth Rendell, Sara Paretsky, Sue Grafton, Patricia Highsmith, Elizabeth George, and Patricia Cornwell. Christie is the most famous and most-widely published mystery writer after Sir Arthur Conan Doyle (Sherlock Holmes). As I write this, Cornwell, George, and Grafton all have books on the *New York Times* bestseller list. Rendell and James have won all of mystery's most prestigious writing awards; Paretsky and Grafton aren't far behind.

♦

Mystery writing has allowed women to present characters—female and male—who step outside the established roles assigned to gender. Christie utilized a variety of detective characters from the elderly village gossip, Miss Jane Marple, to the effete Belgian foreigner, Hercule Poirot. Though many consider Christie too formulaic a craftswoman to be viewed as a serious writer, in fact, she broke many literary taboos in her stories. Her presentation of Poirot, for example, constantly forced Britons to deal with their own ethnocentrism. And Marple is, in many respects, the quintessential feminist hero—a smart, older woman who utilizes her knowledge of life and her attention to a Mary Daly-esque version of gossip to solve crimes.

James, Paretsky, Grafton, and others have added different elements to the mystery formula established by Christie. James writes declaratively political books with both male and female detectives, though her Scotland Yard Inspector Adam Dalgliesh is most famous. But Dalgliesh is a male detective who is, like Dorothy L. Sayers' Lord Peter Wimsey, definingly a feminist creation: driven by internal and personal demons, respectful of women, cynical about the world yet hopeful it can change.

Paretsky and Grafton have revolutionized the female detective first defined by Christie. The genre has featured male detectives in "true" detective roles, that is as police officers or private investigators; women have traditionally been amateur detectives—like Nancy Drew and Miss Marple, they have not had the validation of profession to allow them real credibility as detectives. Paretsky's V.I. Warshawski and Grafton's Kinsey Milhone are both professional private investigators with links to the police; they are credible, no-nonsense, and definingly feminist.

More recently, lesbian writers have added to the expansion of the mystery genre. Katherine V. Forrest and Barbara Wilson have almost single-handedly created a crossover audience among heterosexual readers, with books showcased by Book-of-the-Month Club. Both are award-winning writers; their books have been translated into many languages. Wilson's *Gaudi Afternoon* won a prestigious British Crime Writers Award; Forrest's *Murder at the Nightwood Bar* is currently being made into a film by award-winning director Tim Hunter, starring Mary Louise Parker and Tom Arnold. Both these writers, and the women who have followed their example, have proven that strong female detectives—regardless of their sexual orientation— are compelling for any reader.

The stories in *Out for Blood* follow in the classic feminist tradition of mystery writing. Some are police procedurals, others are tales of suspense, and still others are ghost stories. Most involve murder; all involve the classic models of good and evil, justice and retribution, though these models are not necessarily presented in the classic way.

The contributors come from every area of the United States, are a variety of ages, ethnicities, races, and classes, heterosexual as well as lesbian. Some are new writers; others are established award-winners in the genre. What they have in common is their attention to a feminist vision of mystery and suspense.

Out for Blood includes a variety of detective stories. J.D. Shaw and Kathleen Downey feature male detectives, a Philadelphia police detective and a sheriff from upstate New

York, respectively. In Shaw's story, "A Special Education," sexual harassment on the job takes a deadly turn; in "The Sacrifice," Downey presents a particularly gruesome murder straight from today's headlines and shows how it affects the small town in which it occurs. Like James, both women have crafted male detectives who are fully drawn, eschewing the stereotype of the insensitive male police officer; both men must battle with their own sexism to come to grips with the crimes they must solve.

Katherine V. Forrest and Nikki Baker feature female police detectives. Forrest's now world-famous L.A.P.D. detective Kate Delafield faces sexism and homophobia on the job, but can't escape them on vacation either as murder crosses her path in "Jessie." Cassandra Hope is working her way up in the Chicago P.D.; Nikki Baker's newest detective, premiering here in "Film Noir," must fight race and class barriers in addition to sexism. She also must decide whether justice is best served by the law. Baker, author of the Virginia Kelly series, is one of only a handful of African-American women mystery writers in the U.S.; Cassie Hope is one of the first black women detectives in mystery fiction.

Barbara Wilson also addresses racism and sexism in her story, "An Expatriate Death." International sleuth Cassandra Reilly, who appeared in the award-winning *Gaudi Afternoon* and *Trouble in Transylvania*, finds murder and quite a bit more while vacationing in Mexico. As usual, Wilson brings her keen eye for the visual and the political to bear in Reilly's latest adventure.

But not all women's mystery writing features detectives. Traditionally, the writing of women has focused on the sphere to which women have so often been relegated— domestic life. Many of these stories chart the territory of home, family, and relationships. G.V. Babish's "Rose Fever" examines the most dangerous aspects of male competitiveness—and wifely affection. Lisa D. Williamson's "Home Cookin'" and Linda K. Wright's "American Gothic" uncover the more grisly elements of family life with the darkest of irony. Meredith Suzanne Baird's "The Confectioner" takes revenge on our fat-phobic society and explores the femininization of fat men with gothic humor. Mabel Maney, author of the best-selling Nancy Clue mystery series, applies her quirky view of American life to one of the family's dirtiest secrets in the creepily atmospheric "A Way with Men." The humor is deadly and the atmosphere claustrophobic in Ruthann Robson's postmodernist tale of blighted relationships, "The Pool." Tee A. Corinne's "Predators" is also high on atmosphere, epitomizing every woman's dread of footsteps behind her, and her fear of being victimized—by the known and the unknown. My own story, "An Evening Out," describes a marriage from the vantage point of both wife and husband, detailing how emotional despair can have devastating consequences.

Ghost stories are often our first mysteries—oral tales told at slumber parties or around campfires. Yet ghost stories are traditionally male in tone and author, and often incorporate sexist and racist themes. The four ghost stories in this collection chart new territory. Joanne Dahme's "Weeping Willows" follows the oral—and distinctly female—tradition of tales told by the fireside, featuring two young boys who uncover a grisly secret while visiting the grave of a relative. "The Tree" presents a very benevolent ghost in Ellen S. Korr's romantic tale of a love that will not die. Jewelle Gomez's ghost is also loving in "Merry X-mas," as it struggles to help the protagonist, a young black deaf woman, escape a lonely and isolating world. And the ghosts in Kanani L. Kauka's "Going Home" also are facilitators as they help a young Hawaiian woman combat racism and reclaim her heritage.

These stories are compelling as well as defining in their evocation of the pivotal areas of women's lives. Whether presenting the big-city terrors of victimization that women face or putting a feminist filter on the most mundane aspects of daily life, these tales encompass the variety and diversity of women's mystery writing. And while all these stories are entertaining, they are also deadly serious in the issues they address. But despite a highly politicized foundation, none of these stories is pedantic or didactic; these are stories of the very real—and often quite scary—facets of women's lives.

PREDATORS

Tee A. Corinne

Tessa left the darkroom and paused at the kitchen door, eyes adjusting to the sunlight. Diver, the black labrador retriever, bounded in with big feet and adolescent energy, nosing her, wanting to go for a walk. Doll, the yellow lab, moved with the slowness of age, her tail banging loudly against the side of the oven.

"You're right. It's time to go out," she said as she changed into her walking shoes.

A few minutes later they were in the station wagon, passing the house recently vacated by gun-happy Californians, then passing the cottage where a pit bull guarded the driveway. An encounter with the pit bull was the reason she now drove the dogs up to the Bureau of Land Management forest, instead of walking the easy mile-and-a-half.

The last house on the road had a young family whose parents had just built across the road. Nice people.

No meth labs or marijuana farmers in the area, at least not yet.

Parking in the shade, she locked the car, a precaution that wouldn't have occurred to her when she first moved to this rural Oregonian community, but odd things had happened over the years. She preferred safety to regrets.

Doll and Diver ran happy-dance circles, sniffed the edges of the road, raced up to her, urging her to stop fussing with the car.

The road wound around the mountain. She surveyed the rust-colored cliff that rose on her left, looking for tiny blooming flowers and spotting several. The trees at the top looked dry, a worry at the beginning of fire season. Autumn rains were three or four months away.

To her left, the woods, mostly Douglas fir, dropped off steeply. She hoped whoever had been dumping trash at the top of the road had been caught. Last month she had come upon suitcases, gaping, a whole family's clothing scattered among the pine needles, someone's vacation ruined.

The dogs raced ahead, Doll frolicking like a much younger animal. She guessed it was the smells. Always got them both excited.

Had the police even come to check up on the suitcases? They weren't much help, anyway. The sheriff's office had lost more of its funding, two deputies at night were trying to cover the whole county, and more newcomers were moving up from California, trying to escape the urban crime and drugs, but bringing a lot of it with them. Kids unmanageable. Parents thought if they moved to the country their children would have a better chance. The kids, though, were bored, didn't know how to entertain themselves in a low-tech environment. Shame.

The white fleck of a cigarette stub, ground out at the edge of the road, caught her eye. These newcomers just didn't understand about fire out here. When one starts, houses go up in minutes. No way the fire department could come in time. She hoped the smoker wasn't a regular on the road.

A branch cracked loudly in the trees above her. What would be heavy enough to break a branch like that? Could someone be watching? She couldn't see anything unusual as she scanned the dense growth. Where were the dogs, anyway?

Behind her on the road both dogs stood as if rooted, watching her. Diver ran toward her, hit her with his nose, ran down the road again, and turned to look back at her. A pretty clear message.

"So you want to turn around, big boy?"

Tessa started down the road toward him. Both dogs trotted away from her. Diver, his ears flattened against his head, looked back over his shoulder to make sure she was coming. What could it be? Bear? A big cat of some kind? Elk? She was running too, not knowing from what, running and surveying the trees on the side of the road in case she needed to climb away from an elk.

The bears around were small, wouldn't hurt anyone unless they were wounded. When the dogs slowed to a walk, Tessa did likewise. An old bobcat might attack domestic animals, she guessed, but she thought it would stay away from her.

♦

In the days following Tessa learned that a couple of calves had disappeared under suspicious circumstances, but didn't hear what those circumstances were. Someone thought they had spotted a cougar and a wild animal preserve had lost two panthers, but the preserve was eighty miles away. Her imagination was getting away from her. She feared danger with every noise, every shadow—a log overturned, the shed door ajar.

♦

While Tessa was walking another day, a pale blue truck slowed and pulled alongside, a rifle in the rack behind the driver's head. It was the father from the end of the road.

"Seen anything unusual?" he asked, quieting his own dog with his free hand.

Diver was jumping around with excitement. Doll sat when told to, but Diver had to be held. "The dogs stop about halfway up the road and want to turn back," Tessa said, rubbing Diver's back, tucking his tail and bending his hind legs to make him sit.

The man rubbed sweat from his forehead with a large white handkerchief. "Someone was camping at the turnaround at the top. I took down their license number, but they're gone now." He turned to look out through the trees as if to see who else might be squatting, a common occurrence now that the economy was in a dive.

"Whatever's bothering the dogs up the road, I don't think it's a person. They usually bark at people. This is different. They act scared. Bear or cat is my guess," she said. Diver had calmed down, so she let go of his collar.

"Might be a big cat. A couple of cats and a small dog disappeared recently," the man told her.

Tessa drew in a deep breath. This was not good. "Someone's been smoking along the edge of the road."

"Maybe it's that drifter we had last summer. Saw him back last week. Walks to the top, climbs through the fence, and crosses the freeway, heading north."

"The guy with the Australian shepherd?"

"That's the one." He leaned back, looked at her.

"I saw him in town once. He came out of a store with two ice cream cones. Fed one to the dog."

"Well, let me know if you learn anything," he said, putting the truck into gear.

"You bet," Tessa answered, calling her dogs and heading toward her car.

♦

She felt watched. Every time Tessa went outdoors she had the distinct feeling that someone or something was watching her. Tessa thought it was her imagination or the stories she'd been reading. The *Neighborhood Watch* newsletter warned that a light tan, windowless van had been seen near where several dogs had disappeared. Someone had seen that the inside was filled with animal cages.

Doll was sleeping. Tessa took Diver for a quick walk around the back meadow, rich with the smell of warm leaves and earth. The sun was high, throwing dense but minimal shadows. Tessa and Diver made a circle, starting to the south, crossing two bridges over creeks that were now dry, pausing in the shade of pines to the west. Coming back past the madrone thicket, Diver suddenly became alert. The fur rose all over his body and he leaned away from the area as if both wanting to and being afraid to run. He seemed to move on the tips of his paws. The air was very still. No birds sang.

Tessa moved beside him, afraid to look at the brush too carefully, not wanting to challenge whatever was waiting there.

◆

At the store, later, she asked about large animal sightings.

"A elk got hit on the highway last night. Totalled the car." Several people laughed, but it had not been funny for the driver, who was recuperating in the hospital. A woman told of being confronted on a mountain road by a bull elk. The woman had run to her car and watched as the elk tossed each of her dogs, breaking their necks.

Tessa felt her own neck, hard with tension.

That night she walked the dogs quickly along the driveway. Coyotes laughed in the distance, but they no longer frightened her. Like the rattlesnakes, they were a known quantity. This other thing, though, had gotten under her skin. The whole first year after the divorce she had slept with a light on all night. She decided to do it again.

◆

It was late morning. Walking behind the dogs, Tessa watched their movements, whether they smelled the air or ground. A sweet, soft wind blew off the valley.

The hillside above must have been logged about thirty years earlier. Madrone trees were tall, but not thick, their red, skin-like bark peeled back for summer shedding. Oak, too, and manzanita bushes, with gray-green leaves the size of quarters, clung to the cliff edge. Dry heat rose, making a wet mirage before the turn ahead.

She saw a cigarette butt, ground out, then another, left in the middle of the road, its cool gray ash a frightening indicator of what might have happened to the forest. Who was doing this? She picked up the first butt and read "Marlboro" above the filter. Pocketing it, she walked on.

Ahead of her, Diver came to an abrupt halt, as if hitting an invisible wall. His head was still as his nostrils moved from side to side. Doll paused behind him, nose raised.

"Do you want to go back?" she asked quietly.

Both dogs turned as one and ran, not fast, but steadily back toward the car.

She scanned the hillside, sniffed the air, wished they could tell her what they were noticing. Turning, she ran behind them. Before they reached the car, the dogs had calmed to a walk. What was going on? Was she letting her fears run away with her?

When the dogs reached the car they were acting normal. "Do you want to keep going?" she asked, pointing beyond to a gravel logging road. Diver and Doll almost frolicked toward it. Things couldn't be that bad if the dogs were no longer afraid.

Half a mile up the trail Diver stopped again, nostrils twitching.

She didn't even ask this time, just turned. They jogged together down the hill.

She felt as if her world were being circumscribed, as if there were fewer and fewer places she could go. Perhaps she should drive to the other side of the mountain or over to the quarry. Walk outside the neighborhood for a while.

The evening news carried a story about a junior high school teacher molesting little girls and boys. It was followed, almost editorially, by a comment on a study of homosexual pedophiles. Sometimes she hated living here, the lack of subtlety, the lack of options. A friend back East called to say she's gotten an NEA grant. Tessa wondered if she had made a mistake, choosing to live here, where she could have time to do her own work. Where she could afford that luxury.

Night came and Diver was nervous, jumpy, barking at the door, the window. Whenever she let him out he would look around, then lie down on the walk, watching the road. She heard dogs barking in the distance. There was no hint of moisture in the air. She slept clothed, her shoes and flashlight beside the bed.

✦

In the early afternoon she went to the store for information. Standing near the cash register she drank a

Coke and listened to the CB radio behind the counter, mostly truckers talking about a fire to the north.

Ellie, the proprietor, came over with a rag, cleaning off the road dust.

"You hear about Sam?" she asked, eyes wide, her voice a sultry rasp.

"What about Sam?" Tessa's voice sounded shrill in her ears.

"This morning. Dogs started barking outside. He heard his youngest, the girl, let out a terrible scream. Just started yelling and didn't stop." She paused, shook her head from side to side.

Tessa felt the hair on her body rise. The Coke tasted too sweet in her mouth. She wanted to hurry Ellie. Needed to know, quickly.

"So he grabbed his rifle and ran to the door, and do you know what he saw?" Ellie made change for a customer who then waited to hear the rest of the story.

"Right out there in front of his house the kid was on the ground, screaming. The dogs were holding a tom cougar at bay, keeping that big cat away from the kid."

"Well," she paused and looked around. Everyone was silent, waiting. "Sam shot it." She slammed the countertop for emphasis, making everything rattle, everybody jump.

Ellie paused again, looked out the window into the parking lot. "Don't care if it is illegal to kill them. He had no choice." She rang up another sale. "Hundred-sixty pounds. Full grown." Ellie wiped down the counter, smiled. "Kid's okay."

Tessa shuddered.

The branch cracked in her memory; the white cigarette end caught her eye.

Predators.

She left the store and headed home.

FILM NOIR

Nikki Baker

I

The metal frame begins to rise and give. Lynette Devereaux jerks up hard with both arms on the creaking pull-out couch and eases the old iron legs down softly onto the floor. When the sofa bed is open, she stacks the faded, plaid cushions in a pile over by the desk and stretches out between the cool sheets. Her small brown breasts slope down toward a muscled waist, as tight and trim as a boy's. Thirty-five years old and still no hips, all long, lean leg from below her middle to the size six feet she rubs ritually with a pumice stone in the bath.

Lynette is a creature of ritual, meticulous about her body, her health, her things. Her traveling clothes lie folded on the wooden seat of a desk chair at the periphery of her view. The rest are stacked just as neatly in a bottom dresser drawer left empty for guests in Cassandra Hope's spare bedroom.

Lynette's eyes follow the odd, unfamiliar shadows pitched on the ceiling and the stark white walls. They flicker and bounce like silent pictures. She is listening now for

Many thanks to filmmaker Judith M. Redding, who provided the method for the murder in this story, as well as valuable film insight.

sounds in the cold, dead street. *Now what?* Down the hall
Cassandra is huddled with Luther, her live-in lover. Lynette is
thinking, *What wouldn't you put up with to get what you
want?* Thinking of Luther makes her stomach sour, how
Cassandra has sold herself for a bungalow in Jackson
Park—a middle-class southside Chicago neighborhood,
straight and sanitized even of traffic noises and voices in the
night, sidewalks rolled up, and families tucked in safely, not
much after nine o'clock.

Things change. If little Cassie Hope has remade herself
from a projects scholarship girl into the bourgeoisie, they are
the same in this, remaking what is inconvenient to their
ambition. Lynette guesses her own goals are less obvious,
moving in the opposite direction, from bourgeois princess to
radical African-American filmmaker, nappy-headed lesbian
hoyden. *Hoyden.* Cassandra used to ask Lynette the meaning
of words when they were together, carrying a notebook to
write them down. Weeks later Cassandra would throw them
back in conversation. Lynette wonders if Cassandra does this
still to Luther the lawyer, and doubts it.

What wouldn't you do to get what you want? An
ex-lover posed this question once to Lynette as an almost
criminal indictment. Lynette had been leaving her, clothes
packed in that the self-same dirty, soft-side suitcase now
pushed back under the folding couch. Then, the suitcase was
newer. It was all of it newer when she was leaving Ellen for
Cassandra, ten years ago now. *What wouldn't you do to get
what you want?* The only sensible answer: *Not much.*
Everybody uses everybody else. One big transaction, selling
and being sold.

Thinking of Ellen gives Lynette the shaky feeling she had
as a kid when she'd been caught at something—usually
lying. *What wouldn't you do to get ahead?* Now, Lynette
shakes out the pages of her new script hard before she begins
to read. As she pushes Cassandra out of her mind, a
recollection of Ellen Gilly, squat and jowly on the train from
Philadelphia to Chicago, is there behind it. On the way home
from the train station, Lynette complained to Cassandra how
Ellen had plunked herself down, not next to Lynette exactly,
but deliberately in Lynette's line of sight. Ellen holding her

body like a threat, her lips pursed tight around some sour curse.

Lynette looks up from the script. The words on the page have stopped making sense and her feet are cold. She gulps down the end of the Queen Bee juice from the carton on the nightstand, white stuff in the bottom and all. It still tastes like shit. Cassandra was right about that, but it's raspberry— not Lynette's usual flavor. Sitting up in bed, she gives herself a hug, rubbing her upper arms because it's too much trouble to reach her feet. *Maybe a shower.* It might warm her up.

From the bed, Lynette considers the bath towel folded on the top of the desk for a long while before she braves the chill of the room. The draft is worse than she imagined; nipples standing taut in the cold, she wraps the towel around her breasts. Tucking a corner under her arm, she slips down the hall, closing the bedroom door un-gently. Cassandra and Luther are at the other end of the house, but in the back of her mind she would like to wake them. Even after all these years, Lynette would love to wake Cassandra from this dead suburban sleep, but just now she is willing to settle for the shower.

Her feet sink a little into the spongy rubber mat at the bottom of the tub and burn for a moment under the hot water. But Lynette can feel her body temperature begin to rise, first in her arms and chest, and then down her legs. Bowing her head under the spray, she lets the water drum over her back and shoulders. Steam rolls down from the nozzle like a soft, warm curtain, filling the shower stall with wet, gray air. Eyes closed, Lynette is breathing it in, head back, slicking down her mane of kinky hair in the spray with both hands. Water splatters out a rhythm against the tile and shower glass. It melts against the sides of the tub, washing down in sheets through the shiny, metal spokes of the drain. Legs warm and fluid, Lynette is swaying with the sound of the drumming on the glass, like the swaying rhythm of the train that rocked her to sleep on the long ride from Chicago to Philadelphia.

No.

The swaying in her knees confuses her. The train ride was from Philly to Chicago, for the Gay and Lesbian Film Festival. *Of course.* Her new film, *Dusk*, will be featured

with its first long cut of a bat coming hard and fast out of
the cool spring fog, assaulting the camera, in your face and
mine. "Because queer bashing is personal," she had said to
the *Philadelphia Gay News* in last month's interview. "Why
make it seem like a distant act?" Lynette imagines herself
slouched in the back of the dark screening rooms listening to
the audience's collective gasp. The congratulations are
already ringing in her ears, and of course Lynette has already
spent the prize money.

In the warm running water, the train ride is washed
away. Years melt together. Lynette can almost hear the sound
of Ellen's voice in the roar of the water called up for no
particular reason in the funny way of memory. Or maybe it
is *because* of the shower. Lynette remembers Ellen's
beginning film history class, the steam in her lungs making
her feel all of a sudden light-headed. Her knees sway and
give. In surprise, Lynette lets the soap slide out of her hand.
It skitters along the bottom of the tub as she grabs for the
metal rail on the door of the shower. *Too late.* The door
rattles in its tracks, skidding open, and clanging when it
strikes the wall at the end of its runners. Her ears are ringing
again, this time with the jarring sound of the door hitting
metal, and her palm slides down the smooth white tile,
fingers curling at the ridges in the mildewed grout. She is
falling backward, one hand still closed around the steel gray
bar on the shower door. Her head cracks hard against the
tile, sliding down the wall to the base of the tub, legs buckled
at the knees, heels stopped by the mat on the floor of the
shower. Lynette is sitting. Suddenly sitting again in the class
where she first heard Ellen Gilly, her mentor, talking from
behind a battered, wooden lectern. Years ago, Ellen seemed
to be talking just to her, "Alfred Hitchcock changed the
course of film with his first-person camera in a black-and-
white movie called *Psycho.*"

Now the black writing is coming into focus. It reads:
"The Waterpik by Teledyne," raised letters printed around
the pocked white face of showerhead. Someplace in Lynette's
memory, Ellen is reading from her lecture notes, "Alfred
Hitchcock's *Psycho.* The first post-coital bedroom scene. The
first shot ever of a flushing toilet. A subtle and graphic

depiction of violence that was at once there and not there so as to defy the Hollywood censors."

Lynette understands now, how the odd, fuzzy feeling in her head must be connected to the raspberry-flavored drink she can't remember buying. When she fell asleep on the train, that was when it happened. Now no one will know.

She gropes for the soap, melting somewhere in the water near her hip, without changing position. Stretching by inches, she raises her hand up from the floor of the tub, pressing the dull edge of the soap against the frosted glass. Her arm is heavy as she makes the sweeping motion of the script, two half-circles linked together by a flattened loop. A backward three. At the bottom of the last loop, Lynette's arm falls back into her lap, nicking the soap on the shower runners. She can taste blood in her mouth and her head pounds dully. Lynette would like to sleep, but she raises her hand once more—unsteadily—to trace the second letter, its arc half covering the first. Water rains down in a hard stiff spray against her cheek. From the center of the showerhead, a small, black massage-setting knob stares down at Lynette like the cool objective eye of a camera.

II

Cassandra believes for a moment that she can hear water running faintly above the ringing in her ears. Waking light-headed from a strangely heavy sleep, Cassandra is together enough to recognize she is not thinking clearly. Still, without opening her eyes she can tell it is early from the sounds in the street. Six o'clock. *Maybe.* Every day Cassandra makes thousands of pedestrian deductions, what time it is before looking at her watch, who is at the door, who it will be when the phone rings. She makes them self-consciously, a guessing game, applauding her own unremarkable accuracy, keeping sharp for her next promotion. Only a few more years. Cassandra can hear it now from memory in the mouths of disappointed lovers, all of her life as a question: *Why are you so driven?*

How can Cassandra say it, except that she wants something more than what folks think she ought to have. But Luther, here in the bed beside her, never asks. This is one of the things Cassandra likes about him, besides his job, his shiny silk Italian suits, his crisp, flawless diction, and his elaborately folded pocket handkerchiefs. She imagines Luther appreciates her ambitions or at least her pragmatism.

Ten years ago Cassandra had been teaching second grade in the public schools for twenty-one thousand dollars a year, sleeping with girls and being introduced to no one more influential than a class of angry kids stopped for a hot minute on their way to crack cocaine and gang warfare. That was before Cassandra figured out that the Police Academy was paying thirty-two grand to go to school with showcase assignments for the early classes of women cops and your picture in the local paper. Five years to make detective in the Department's first wave of affirmative action, sergeant in another two years, and now this lawyer man with his place in Jackson Park isn't bad for a not-so-pretty, not-so-special girl from the clapboard squalor of Chicago public housing.

In the familiar heat of Luther's body, Cassandra knows by the light and the shortness of the shadows across the door, that the clock radio will very soon begin to sway with the rhythms of a soft jazz instrumental and the suave-voiced patter of the radio morning man. As it does, she can hear Luther groan predictably. He turns, hugging her back to his hairless chest, and his musky smell catches her in waves. Cassandra doesn't need to turn to know that Luther's skin is shining as if someone oiled it. His face shines too, the color of wet Georgia clay. She has traced the hills of his nose and cheeks, the expression lines that run in gullies at the sides of his mouth, and eyelashes so long they belong on a girl. For all these charms, Luther is not an observant man.

This ability to look the other way has made Luther first chair assistant State's Attorney, the only black man in the office with more than ten years. He is oblivious to the outbound progression of brown faces through the State's Attorney's revolving door, doesn't notice the sickly trickle of brothers going the other way. If he noticed how few black men had made it, it would surely make him too sick to glad-hand those Chicago ethnics. Surely he must not see, and so Luther remains their token, keeps hold of the power to make Cassandra into what she wants—a token too.

The same way Luther has managed to look right through his glass ceiling, he has just as expertly missed the signs that their relationship is fraying, clues in the way Cassandra's eyes wander as they stand together at parties that soon she will be on her way. Luther must have forgotten how they met.

He kisses her neck, and sighs. Sitting up stiffly, he sets his feet on the floor with a slap. Cassandra listens for his padding down the hall. A big man, Luther chooses his clothing carefully for grace, but naked he is lumbering, rough flats of his feet smacking the floor boards. Today his heavy step is preceded by the rustle of his bathrobe being pulled from the hook behind the door, and Cassandra is reminded that they have a house guest. Down the hall there is water still running. She thinks it is strange for Lynette to be awake so early.

Stretching to reach it, Cassandra downs what is left of a flat, brown soda from the glass on the floor, then rolls over again, hugging her arms across her chest. Her head hurts. Who knows how much time has passed before Luther is shaking her hard by the shoulder and shouting, "Cassie, will you get up."

But her limbs are heavy and she is mumbling back, "Not yet. What time is it?" Eyes still closed.

When she finally opens them, Luther's face is shining anxiously. Perspiration is beading up between his lip and the manicured fringe of his mustache. "Cassie," he says, "that friend of yours is all passed out in the shower."

Then, Cassandra can hear it clearly, the sound of water, and somehow she is trotting down the hall bare-assed with her tee shirt flapping, and cursing, wondering aloud why the dumb motherfucker hasn't bothered to turn off the water.

When Cassandra opens the bathroom door, Lynette Devereaux is curled like a baby in the tub with her eyes closed and her head cracked open. There is a smear of blood from the top of the tile down to the crown of her head and a weakly colored pool of water where her hips and shoulders have dammed up the back of the tub. Her knees are tucked to her chest and the water rolls over the bend of her hip, through the coarse stiff hair between her legs. A light, cold spray flies out of the open shower door.

God. Cassandra turns both knobs together hard, and the
pipes shudder and sigh as the water goes off. Standing one
foot ankle-deep in the tub of pink water, Cassandra pries
Lynette's fingers from around a slimy bar of white soap,
turns Lynette's arm wrist up and presses two fingers against
the artery. *No pulse.* The firm brown skin Cassandra used to
touch has turned the color of an old black eye. The fingertips
that made love to her are wrinkled and pursed; the arms that
held Cassandra are stiff.

Now Cassandra is yelling in a hoarse, morning voice for
Luther, who is slow in coming to help her move Lynette.
Together, they lift the body by either arm and flop it in the
center of the room on its stomach like a heavy sack. A weak
stream of red trickles out of the nose and runs across the
bathroom floor. Cassandra can feel last night's supper in her
throat, coming back. But her mouth is too dry at first when
she tries to spit. Bent over the sink, she rinses her mouth and
spits again. In the mirror, her reflection has sallow skin and
glassy eyes, their sockets filling with tears. Her grief-tight
throat won't make a sound.

"Shit," Luther says. In the mirror Cassandra can see him
standing behind her, his yellow suspenders hanging at his
thighs. Luther calls them "braces," with a pretension she
finds annoying. Odd because Cassandra has always liked
pretensions. She has arranged her life to rub up against
people who have them, this up-and-coming neighborhood,
this well-mannered professional man. They are supposed to
insulate her from ugliness, let her relegate it to police
business hours and other people's lives.

His hands are around her shoulders. They squeeze
open-close, open-close, in a peaceful rhythm that nearly puts
her back to sleep. Luther's hands are always warm. "Are you
all right?" His fingers open again and drop away.

Is she all right? *Who the hell knows?* The PD took the
horror out of corpses years ago. But Lynette's accident brings
it home, brings Cassandra down into dirt and disorder, same
as she thought she left when she left the projects. Guilty for
thinking it is just like Lynette to leave her in an emotional
mess, Cassandra would like to get angry about it, but she
feels too numb in her feet and hands, as if she's been
drinking, morning-after drunk with a mind too empty to call

up even sadness. This, she imagines, is shock, and the
plausibility of this explanation comforts her. She keeps
thinking the pain will come later; she braces herself.
Cassandra is still waiting for it to hit when the police and
paramedics arrive. They gently move her out of the way of
their business. After a while, they carry Lynette away on a
stretcher under a clean white sheet. Somebody ought to call
her people. Cassandra knows Lynette has a mother living in
Philadelphia. She has met her awkwardly at a big house in
Mount Airy—Mrs. Devereaux an imposing woman, smiling
stiffly, appraising Cassandra's inferior class evidenced by her
cheap, blue, teacher's-salary dress, blaming Cassandra
mutely in over-politeness for her daughter's habits—her
word for Lynette's lesbianism. She will no doubt blame
Cassandra for this accident as well. The slight is worse
because Lynette was born with everything Cassandra
wants—recalling all the other slights, other conversations
with people who don't think Cassandra is worth shit. Just
the thought of the house on Pelham Road still fills
Cassandra's throat with bile.

"What is it exactly you do, Cassandra?" Then, nodding,
"Oh. A teacher," meaning those who *can, do*. Mrs.
Devereaux folds her hands in her lap and smiles with her lips
held tight together. She asks, "Where did you say that you
met her, Lynette?"

There will be an address book in Lynette's things, but
Cassandra hasn't got the heart to look through them now.

"Are you all right?" Luther has managed to put his
jacket on. She hates it that he has found the time to dress,
even to dress fashionably. "Cassie?" he asks, and she feels
her knees give out before she can think of where to sit down.

Her eyes go out too as if someone has turned off the
lights. In the darkness she can hear Luther swearing gently
under his breath. "Jesus." And there is a sudden, sharp pull
at her shoulder. "Goddamn it." Luther has her by the arm,
breaking her fall. She can feel him lose hold, then catch her
again with a jerk. He is cradling her with his body now,
squatting, her back supported by his knees in his expensive
trousers. There is his musky cologne and the comfortable
heat of his breath against her face. His shouting sounds as if

he is talking under water. Luther's breath smells of coffee, and Cassandra could sleep forever.

III

At ten o'clock Ellen Gilly has just accepted the complimentary breakfast that comes with her room. It seems to her like all the sweet luxuries that have been missing from her life. A tall, dark boy sets up the tray and she tips him so well that he snaps to attention, smiling wide before he puts the money away.

When he has gone, Ellen settles herself in the place he has set for her on a high, round coffeetable by the television. She raises her orange juice and closes her eyes as she swallows, thinking of sugar. Ellen has missed dinner, but with all the adrenalin, the excitement of this trip, she hasn't felt it yet.

Beside her continental breakfast plate she has laid out the large blue pill. It strikes her as fitting that the pill is the size and shape of a shortened bullet. She holds it in her open hand, peering down through the rectangle at the bottom of her bifocals. The bifocals are a new development, like the gray hair, the stubborn fat that seemed to grow up in rolls overnight on her butt and belly, and the diabetes that necessitates the big blue pills. All of it goes to show you can't escape what you were born into; that and the talk about exercise, education, hard work, talent, and advancement is a crock. The blue bullet shows that it all comes down to who you are, who you know, lucky connections, lucky DNA. There hasn't been much luck of either kind in Ellen Gilly's life. The world is rigged to go against people like Ellen, fat and sorry and black. But if you can't fuck the system, you can sure as hell fuck up the winners. The winners have gone out of their way to do the same to her.

In Lynette Devereaux's review for the film magazine *8-16-35-70*, she wrote of Ellen's newest film, "Why make another girl-meets-girl? Why make another black-girl meets white-girl in particular when the emphasis in our community should be on women of color loving each other?" Ellen thinks, the abiding love of a knife in the back. Later, Lynette had asked, "Would you rather I'd have let the magazine ignore *Culture Shock*," Ellen's film treatment of an Ann

Allen Shockley novel. "Because," Lynette had said smugly, "they would have." Rubbing the slight in Ellen's face, "They would have looked the other way, pretended you hadn't made a film at all, or put out some review that was more retrospective than critical." So, Lyn did Ellen the favor of writing instead, "Ellen Gilly has spent a career holding the place for gay work to come. Now it's time for her to step aside gracefully." Friendly advice. Another unkind cut in a series of cuts and slights and rejections, some professional, some not. All of them coming down to who was younger, prettier, better copy.

Lynette's editor had known the hip, bitchy style made good ink. "What would you have had me do," Lynette had asked her, "compromise my artistic integrity?" when Ellen stopped her in the aisle of the train to tell her what she thought.

Integrity. Ellen smiles bitterly through a second swallow of orange juice just behind the pill. She has six more pills left, counting the one she has just taken. The rest are gone, nearly three month's prescription spilled, she will have to tell Dr. Golden, in the bathroom on the train. "All that rocking." She will have to ask Dr. Golden for some more when she gets home to Philadelphia, admitting that injecting herself with the insulin in her bag which he has encouraged her to try makes her squeamish. She must make due with the Diabinese and discipline herself to keep a careful watch on her condition. Dr. Golden, a white man young enough to be her son, always smiles at the matronly voice with which she resigns herself to his ministrations. "Well, Dr. Golden, the body ages."

The body ages. Youth passes away—and lovers, and fame. So perhaps it's just the way things go that, knocking on the door of fifty-two years old, Ellen Gilly has had all of these that the world will give her. But over the last sweet swallow of her orange juice Ellen Gilly wonders what Lynette Devereaux is doing this morning, Lynette Devereaux who is young, marginally talented, predatory, and unkind. Lynette Devereaux who is lucky, too, in a way she does not deserve to be, or worse, doesn't even fully appreciate. Lynette Devereaux believes it is her right to be rich and famous, and Ellen's lot to eat her dust. Not if Ellen can help it.

Over the silt in the bottom of her juice glass, Ellen Gilly wonders when Lynette Devereaux who is rising so high so fast will come upon her limits, failing youth, failing health, failing talent, the inevitable blue bullet meant for her. Six bullets left in Ellen's prescription bottle, like Russian roulette, a game of limits. One bullet and five empty chambers. But Ellen would like to see Lynette get even odds.

IV

Lynette Devereaux is dead. *Dead*, Cassandra is thinking, waking up in a white room, under antiseptic-smelling linen in a bed with high steel sides and an intravenous drip. If that isn't bad enough, her head is pounding, the dull ache she gets when she doesn't eat. In the sterile, windowless room she has no idea at all what time it is, and no guess either.

"I didn't expect you to need a stretcher too." The joke is strained. Not even Luther, who tells it, is laughing. The ridge of his brow scrunches up his eyes. The lines age his face and Cassandra wonders if this is what he will look like in twenty years.

"What happened?" She remembers about Lynette and feels sick again, but her thoughts are still strangely empty. She asks him blankly, "What time is it?" watching his expression carefully for signs that there is something wrong with her—something other than shock.

Luther blinks once, twice. He rubs his face as he explains how she fainted. Good thing, he says, that the paramedics were still around. He looks away and down at something she cannot see on the floor by his chair. "I packed you a change of clothes and some personal things in a bag here." This is not surprising. She was wearing nothing but a tee-shirt when she passed out. Luther is never thrown off his game. A master of protocol, as a black man, his basic survival skill is perfection.

Luther pauses, sucking his lip before he tells her, "The doctor asked me if you were pregnant." Cassandra can see that Luther is asking too. He is staring at her.

Pregnant. The word wakes her up into the life her mother had. Cassandra stares back.

"I'm not pregnant," she says. "What time is it anyway?"

Luther's shoulders relax. He looks down at the face of the brand new, 40's-style watch underneath his starched French cuff. It is almost noon. Leaning over the rail of the hospital bed, he kisses Cassandra. She can see a baby blue uniform in the doorway, across the back of his stark white shirt. The short, solid young policeman has a hairless face the complexion of chalk. He looks at the floor until Luther lets Cassandra go.

"Excuse me." The officer smiles. Cassandra smiles too. If she tried to buy a house in Cicero, he and his friends would throw a brick through her window, burn a cross on her lawn. Her partner Lonnie Hudson likes to say that joining the Chicago PD is the same as going South, because it turns black folks into "our niggers" and "their niggers."

Luther straightens, rolling his shoulders. He adjusts the legs of his trousers carefully and then his tie. The white boy stands at the side of the bed like he ought to salute, but he keeps his hands clasped together at his back. Today Cassandra is one of "our niggers." One of our head niggers. They both watch Luther slip his suit jacket off the back of the visitor's chair. Everybody knows Luther; he's the black guy at the State's Attorney. "How's it going, Counselor?" The officer walks over to shake Luther's hand.

"Not bad. Treat her right." Luther is shoving an arm through the sleeve of his suit jacket, stiffly. He doesn't like to advertise their thing. Luther picks up his long camel coat from the foot of the bed and smoothes it across his arm.

When the back of his suit has disappeared through the doorway, the officer sits, knees creaking as he lowers himself into the empty visitor's chair. He takes the pencil from behind his ear and lifts his behind again just slightly, feeling for the pad of paper in his back pants pocket before he starts to talk. There is not much to say. He would like some background for his report, who Lynette was, why she was at Cassandra's house. His pencil is ready on the open pad.

Cassandra has known Lynette since she went to Temple University. Lynette was at Philadelphia U, sleeping with her film professor, Ellen Gilly. Cassandra was coming out, cautiously. She haunted the gay bookstore, Giovanni's

Room. Then after she met Lynette, Cassandra didn't need to read about women anymore.

Lynette left Ellen about the time Cassandra left Temple with her degree in elementary education. They tried to make it, and couldn't. Lynette moved on, moved up to someone else more like herself. It hurt. Cassandra moved back to Chicago. That was the end of it. They had stayed in touch. Barely.

"Lynette Devereaux was a friend of the family," the officer begins to write what Cassandra tells him, "From Philadelphia. I knew her years ago at college. She was here in Chicago for a visit."

"A visit," he repeats. His lips move as if he is spelling to himself.

Cassandra pauses. "Or something. Lynette didn't really say."

V

At home again Cassandra strips to her panties in front of the bathroom mirror, pulls her robe off the hook behind the door and holds it for a moment, examining the line of muscle in her thighs. Her body pleases her. At thirty-four it is still tight, no stretch marks, and no wrinkles on her ageless face, only laugh lines at the sides of her mouth to give it character. Cassandra splashes water from the sink up toward her cheeks with both hands. At thirty-four she is still alive.

She would like a shower, but not until she has scrubbed down the tub, the floor, and the walls too. The steam from the foaming water in the plastic bucket smells like pine as Cassandra bends close, moving her thick pink sponge across the linoleum floor in widening circles, scrubbing hard at nothing she can see. She stands barefoot on the spongy rubber mat at the bottom of the tub, working her way down the shower screen. The sponge cuts an easy swathe through the scum on the glass. At the bottom where the glass meets porcelain, there is a heavy squiggle of caked, dried soap. The cracking lines spell out a backward 3 and the letter O. Squatting down in the tub, Cassandra rubs hard until the shower glass comes clean. When she's done, the whole room smells sharp and bitter.

Lynette's things are still down the hall in the spare room. Cassandra sits on the floor by the empty liquor box she has brought from the garage to pack them up and ship them. Where? To Lynette's steely-eyed mother? She opens the dresser's flimsy, press-board drawers and closes them again. The fold-out couch is still open with the sheets turned back on one side, looking fresh, Cassandra thinks, un-used. The light on the nightstand is on and a script is laid open across the top of a brown overnight bag. It's too early in the year for the nights to have gotten long, and Cassandra can't imagine why Lynette had started her shower in the middle of the night. She picks up the script and reads the title, *Dusk*. She turns it over, running her fingers around the edges of a red blotch on the back of the pages. The stain is dried now, still just barely sticky. There is an empty carton of the Queen Bee health drink Lynette likes—used to like—in the trash, and two more cartons turned on their sides at the bottom of her bag. Their clear plastic bottoms are sticky too, with the same dried red goo as in the bag.

Cassandra runs her hands along the tops and bottoms of the cartons, but they are dry. She carries them to the kitchen and wipes down their sides with a dishrag, feeling very tired, before she puts them away in the refrigerator. She will deal with Lynette's things tomorrow. Cassandra stretches out on the couch for a minute and as soon as her back hits the cushions, she is asleep again and dreaming.

Cassandra is dreaming of Lynette Devereaux, naked in a shower filled with steam, wet-mouthed and pulling Cassandra underneath the spray, eyes closed. Making love in the shower. It is almost like remembering. Her hands feel warm between Cassandra's legs, and Cassandra is urging the fingers deeper, pushing Lynette's hand until the fingers won't go any further into her, and the hand she is pressing is limp and cold. When Cassandra opens her eyes she is holding a corpse with Luther's face. As she screams, the corpse slips away, falling backward, staring open-mouthed. His head splits open against the tile, and diamonds spill out instead of brains, glittering as they catch the light. On the shower mat the diamonds clump and bead together like drops of water, like writing on a clean, white piece of paper.

♦

In the morning the room is bright and Cassandra wakes up in her own bed. Luther is shaking her and her head hurts. He is already dressed for work, looking earnestly into her face. She tells him, "EO," the pattern the diamonds wrote out in her dream.

"What?" Luther presses a broad, cool hand against her forehead like her mother used to do. "Are you sick?" He scrunches up his face and peers back into hers intently. "You were asleep on the couch when I got home last night. I woke you up and made you eat." He asks, "Don't you remember?"

Cassandra doesn't. She doesn't even remember what day it is. The red numbers of her alarm clock read eight-twenty-five, Wednesday.

"You look sick," Luther pronounces again, kissing her on the forehead quickly. "Call in—all right?" he says, "You promise?" Holding Cassandra's chin in his hand, he nods her head for her, yes, up and down. "Stay home today."

But as soon as Cassandra hears the front door close she is up and pulling her yellow silk blouse off its hanger. She is down the hall, curling her chemical-smooth hair with a heated wand. It is the writing, E.O., on the shower that bothers her. People who have had accidents use their energy to scream or call for help—not to write initials. *People don't take showers in the middle of the night.* Cassandra remembers the new white bath mat she put at the bottom of the tub for company, and wonders if Lynette really slipped at all. Dressed, she takes her gun from the drawer in the nightstand and slips it into the shoulder harness. Cassandra folds the jacket of her pants suit over an arm and wears her heavy winter coat bunched up around her in the car. She goes two blocks, makes a left onto South Shore, and heads for the Medical Examiner's office at Harrison and Leavitt by the University of Illinois.

VI

Cassandra is going to see Solange Orstrowski, a med tech she knows from the PD. A skinny little bird of a woman, she makes up for her size in swagger and competence. Solange is a dyke, everybody knows. It is written all over her. Nobody knows about Cassandra, except Solange, and maybe Luther, maybe Cassandra's partner, Hudson. Solange was a mistake, two years ago for a while when Cassandra was lonely. Cassandra was working Juvenile Hall and Solange picked her up over lunch at Dragomento's. Cassandra didn't make it back to her shift that day, fun and games. Solange didn't see it that way and things fizzled out after a couple more lunches. But Cassandra likes Solange; she's honest, no bullshit. Lonnie Hudson kids Cassandra, "Seems like Sally O. is always wanting to do you a favor."

"So?" Cassandra tells him, "Lonnie, honey, you can't have too many friends."

Cassandra finds Solange smoking at her desk. At the ME's office, everybody smokes. Someone, maybe Solange, told Cassandra once that it helps to take the taste away at autopsies. Cassandra just waits until Solange looks up. Solange blows out hard toward the desktop and puts her cigarette down in an ashtray that is really a coffee saucer, full of yellowing butts. When the saucer is clean, there are two delicate Polish dancers in wide, pleated skirts swirling along the bottom, holding hands like girlfriends. Solange picks up her cigarette and stubs it out in the dish with the others, blows more smoke up over her head, putting on her old Chicago, Bridgeport, accent. "And how are you, fine Lady Sergeant?"

"I'm making it," Cassandra says, but her head still hurts.

"Uh huh." The gap in Solange's front teeth shows when she smiles. Her green-blue eyes with their lazy lids run down Cassandra's clothes and up again, an exaggerated appraisal. "Yeah, I see that." Solange laughs easily at herself. "And what can I do you out of?" The Bridgeport accent is gone, smoothed out into something vaguely "Chicagoland," unidentifiable by neighborhood within twenty miles of O'Hare Airport, as she lights another cigarette from the battered pack by the picture of her little dog, a Yorkshire terrier called Muffin, that she keeps on her desk. Solange likes her friends to call her Sal, so Cassandra does.

"Sal." Cassandra leans across the desk and tells her, "A woman slipped in my shower yesterday. She hit her head and died." There is a catch Cassandra had not expected in the back of her throat. It stops her for a moment, before she can add, "She was a friend of mine."

Behind the smoke, interest seems to have turned Solange's eyes from green to a washed-out teal. She brushes away the wispy blond hair that has fallen in front of them.

Cassandra says, "I have a feeling something made her slip."

"Like what?" Solange is nodding and writing while she listens. The cigarette hanging from her lips makes long, precarious ash.

That's the thing. Cassandra doesn't know. She says, "I put a brand new bath mat on the bottom of the tub before she came to stay, and I found the letters E and O written on the shower door in soap while I was cleaning up. I think she knew she was going to die, and she wanted to tell me something."

Solange doesn't say anything, just keeps writing. Cassandra is waiting for the ash at the end of her cigarette to fall. She tells Solange, "I was wondering if you'd run some blood work for me, as a favor." Her hand touches Sal's across the desk and Sal stops writing. Reaching out to tap away her ash, she leaves the cigarette burning in the dirty saucer.

"Let me show you something." Sal bends over in her chair and points to a stack of papers on the floor behind her desk. "You see this? These are my back reports for filing." She slaps the pileup in her metal in-box. "And these are my requests for blood work." Sal would like to help her, really, but if the investigating officers are thinking accidental death, then take a number. Sal is looking hard at Cassandra as she asks, "Hypothetically, how do you know the soap on the shower door has anything to do with her dying? How do you know she didn't just slip and mark up the glass by accident on her way down? It's a bitch if she was your friend and all, I know. But I've got babies turning up in garbage cans. It's going to be hard to justify forensics on somebody who maybe just slipped in the shower, you know?"

What can Cassandra say? That the marks were two low on the glass for that; the marks are gone. It makes Cassandra feel even more foolish to hear the pity in Sal's voice, as if she's losing future credibility even with Sal, which she can't afford.

"If you come up with anything else," Sal says, meaning anything better, "you can call me. Hell, Cassie, you could call me anyway. Maybe next week about the blood work. I'll try, all right? Take it easy, Cassandra," Sal puffs out charitably, "you look tired."

Cassandra *is* tired. She's been beat since she woke up. The walk down the long beige hall to double glass doors seems longer going than coming. It gives Cassandra time to wonder who else she can hit up for a favor. She keeps wondering all the way down the front walk to the street.

On Lake Shore Drive, it's almost as if Cassandra is looking in from the outside of her body. But the car rolls on straight ahead. Out over the lake, the clouds are gray and close to the water. In the far distance, a puff of white smoke rides on the stack of a tugboat and Cassandra is thinking of Solange. Her small steely body, everything hard but her moist tobacco kisses. Everything cool but the sudden laugh that opens Sal's face sometimes when they are alone. At the edges of her voice even now, Cassandra can feel her fondness and her shy confusion underneath the perennial tough. No hard feelings, the same old same old. Same old Solange after months now since they have touched, the sweet expectant familiarity of old lovers, now careful friends.

Cassandra is squinting to make out the detail of the tug, but it's getting harder to keep her eyes open; the lower she lets her eyelids drop, the harder it gets. The circle of black water around the tug keeps closing in until after a while everything is black and Cassandra's floating out over the middle of the lake on that puff of smoke. The car seems to roll along on its own in the lane by the rail where Cassandra has started it until suddenly the air around her is full of sound. When she can finally open her eyes again she is skidding along the center divider, throwing orange and yellow sparks at the guard rail like the head of a comet on a trail of white paint. Horns are blaring when the car finally comes to a stop. Behind her someone is shouting, "Get an ambulance," but before Cassandra can see who it is, her eyes are closed again.

VII

Cassandra wakes up in another white room. She would swear it's the same one she left less than 24 hours before. But instead of four clean white walls, this one has a window. Outside the light is getting thin. Her arm is sore, and she can see a purple bruise where they have taken blood.

Instead of Luther in the chair beside the bed, there is a bald, white doctor in a stained lab coat shaking a finger at her. The doctor has a doughy, red face that is mostly forehead. Two veiny, blue eyes are set just about in the middle of it. He says his name is Dean, talking patiently, the way people speak to children.

He tells her how lucky she is. "You could have been killed." Dr. Dean pulls a chart from the foot of her bed and reprises the entries quickly. "Passed out yesterday morning. Passed out today behind the wheel. Hypoglycemic. That means your blood sugar was low. That's why you passed out." He chides her with the same brisk bedside cheerfulness, "Miss Hope, diabetics have got to keep that sugar up."

"I'm not diabetic," Cassandra says.

Looking down at the chart again, the doctor rubs the shiny red skin on the top of his head as if this is not what he expected. "Has this ever happened before?" he asks.

"Yesterday." Cassandra's thoughts are still unsteady, but she seems to remember. "I was here yesterday."

"I can see that." The doctor's words are running together, but Cassandra can't tell whether this is the fault of his talking or her listening. His questions seem to come at her rapid-fire. "Any fainting before yesterday? When was the last time you ate? Any history of liver problems? Are you taking drugs?" he asks, writing her answers carefully in the chart, "because if you're taking drugs and you don't tell us, it could be very bad." He is peering across the bed tray worry-faced, "Ms. Hope? Are you all right?"

Cassandra wonders. She is feeling faint again and her vision has begun to narrow.

"Are you all right?" the doctor repeats. Cassandra is not sure. He pushes the shallow, plastic cup of orange juice the nurse has left across the bed tray and orders her to drink it.

The juice seems to help. Cassandra is thinking now. Remembering the swaying sensation in her knees and the strange tunnel vision when she blacked out in the car, it occurs to her that something must be very wrong. Remembering writing on the door and Lynette curled up in the tub with the soap in her fist, Cassandra wonders if this doesn't somehow prove that something was wrong with Lynette as well. *EO. Too late.* Cassandra doesn't want to end up like Lynette.

Cassandra asks, "Could a drug do this—something with the name 'EO?'"

"Not EO," the doctor shrugs, "but if you were taking someone else's insulin—that would certainly be the easiest explanation. Or maybe Orinase, I don't know, Diabinese." He is mumbling to himself. "But why would you have gotten into that?"

Cassandra's brain is working slowly, like a rusty machine, but she is getting there. *Not something, someone.* Cassandra remembers how the letters overlap. *Not EO, EG.* The loop of the G was sloppy and almost closed, but she knows what Lynette was writing now—the name of the woman Lynette said had it in for her. "Look," Cassandra says, "could someone have drugged me?"

Dr. Dean is looking past her, smiling faintly. Cassandra wishes she had her badge to prove to the doctor that her suspicions are valid, official. His expression takes her back to when she was a girl, led in a long line of pickaninnies by some earnest-faced woman teacher narrating every block of a city where Cassandra has spent her whole life like a guide on a double-decker tourist bus. "This is the Field Museum built for the World's Fair in 1933," pointing at the skyline, "and to your left, children, is the Sears Tower, the tallest building in the world, and the Prudential building." Lake Michigan was less than thirty blocks away, and ten-year-old Cassandra had never seen it, never seen much of anything that wasn't the cinderblock hot dog stands in her neighborhood and the urban bazaar on Maxwell Street, buying stolen hub caps from a table set up on the street beside boxes full of underwear seconds.

"Now why do you think someone would want to drug you?" Dr. Dean asks, still smiling his well-meaning condescension. "Something you need, Ms. Hope?"

"My purse." She points to it on the chair near the window. Her badge is still there in the inside zippered pocket, and someone has taken her gun from the shoulder holster and put it inside the purse too. With her badge in her hand Cassandra feels more like herself again, flipping open the cover of the small black wallet and flashing the silver shield. "I don't know, Dr. Dean, why or even if someone wants to drug me," she tells him. "But I think we'd better try to find out."

♦

The blood work takes about three hours and they keep Cassandra at the hospital for observation. She has told Luther not to come. He's in trial so he doesn't, but he calls twice anyway just to have her tell him she's fine. When the drug screen comes back, the doctor brings the results himself, rubbing his palms together expectantly. "Ms. Hope, the good news is we know why you've been passing out. The bad news is that there's enough Diabinese in your system to kill you. Now all we have to do is to find out how it got there."

All Cassandra knows is that she could have ended up like Lynette in the shower, going to sleep and not waking up. The thought makes her nauseous again. "Slow down," she says, "and tell me what this is."

Rolls of red skin pile up on Dr. Dean's forehead as he frowns. "Well, Diabinese is a drug that works like insulin. I can't think of any reason anyone would take it for recreation. It's used mostly for milder, late-onset diabetes. Insulin has to be injected, but Diabinese is taken orally, in pills." He is rubbing the stubborn dimple in his chin. "I'll have to ask you again, Detective Hope. If you've been taking anyone else's medication for any reason, I need to know."

"What do you think?" Cassandra thinks Dr. Dean wouldn't be saying this if she were a rich, white, Lake Forest housewife. She stares at him until he clears his throat, looking back down at his test results.

"Diabinese stays in your system longer than insulin, sometimes days. If you stopped eating or were eating very little or were under stress, you'd tend to pass out like you did. Generally, you'd need some sugar to revive you, but depending on how much you'd ingested, chances are you might not wake up at all." Dr. Dean isn't smiling any more, and it looks to Cassandra as if he is beginning to consider what she already believes. "I'd just recommend that you eat three big, square meals a day for the next week or so, and check in with your internist. Of course the real question remains," Dr. Dean says more slowly, as if he's thinking this out as he's saying it, "how you got into the stuff in the first place."

Cassandra is thinking of E.G. *Ellen Gilly.* "Don't worry about that," she says. "That's my job."

VIII

At home Cassandra calls Luther from the phone in the kitchen to give him the message that Import & Domestic Motor Works thinks his car is unsalvageable, making herself a ham and cheese sandwich and chugging coca-cola from the two-liter bottle. She likes that the Diabinese has given her a mandate to eat like a horse.

"Never mind about the goddamn car," Luther tells her. "I've got court today and I don't think I can cancel it. But I can get someone to come over and sit with you, unless you're sure you're all right."

"I've been better," Cassandra says, mouth full. "But I've been worse." She doesn't really have time to talk to Luther right now. She is bending over the kitchen counter, reading the copy of the *Physicians' Desk Reference* Luther uses to prepare for his trials. The text says

DIABINESE (chlorpropamide), is an oral glucose-lowering drug of the sulfonylurea class. . . . Chlorpropamide is a white crystalline powder that has a slight odor. It is practically insoluble in water. . . . It is soluble in alcohol..

"You know, maybe we could take a little vacation," Luther proposes. "Maybe Hawaii."

Cassandra is nodding into the phone between her shoulder and cheek, still reading.

DIABINESE exerts a hypoglycemic effect in normal humans within one hour, becoming maximal at 3 to 6 hours and persisting for at least 24. . . . Severe hypoglycemic reactions with coma, seizure, or other neurological impairment occur infrequently, but constitute medical emergencies requiring immediate attention. . . . Patients should be closely monitored for a minimum of 24 hours since hypoglycemia may recur after apparent clinical recovery.

The thought that she has nearly died almost puts Cassandra off her food, but not quite. She opens the door of the fridge and reaches for a second helping of cheese. On the shelf inside the refrigerator door where the Coke goes is a carton of Lynette's Queen Bee juice.

"Bee pollen always helps keep my energy up when I travel." Lynette had asked Cassandra, "Does this taste funny to you? I don't usually buy raspberry."

"This must be healthy. It tastes like medicine," Cassandra remembers complaining. "It tastes like hard raspberry cider." Tracing back up the page with her finger Cassandra finds the entry she has just read:

Chlorpropamide is a white crystalline powder that has a slight odor. It is practically insoluble in water. . . . It is soluble in alcohol.

Cassandra remembers the other juice cartons, the ones in the spare room. *That's how Ellen Gilly did it.* Rummaging in her purse on the counter for her compact, she flips open the little plastic shell and runs the magnifying mirror over the cartons of Queen Bee juice, squinting for holes.

"I've got a friend with a time share on Kaui," Luther tells her. "Beach front. We could get some champagne and do that *From Here to Eternity* thing."

"Can't wait, baby," Cassandra tells Luther, "but how about I call you back later?"

Cassandra drops the phone back in its cradle on the wall, turns the juice container upside down on a paper towel, and breaks the ice cubes out of a fresh tray before she pours herself another Coke. Cassandra can imagine how it went now, see it all played out. Ellen Gilly, a jilted lover, a beaten rival, sitting across the aisle of the train all the way from Philadelphia plotting it. She can almost see Ellen Gilly's eyes sliding up over the pages of a glossy magazine, watching for her chance. In the compact mirror, Cassandra thinks she can make out a nick in the top of the carton, just barely. She gathers a handful of plastic freezer bags from the second drawer below the silverware and takes them with her down the hall to the spare room. One empty juice carton is still in the trash can. Cassandra picks it up carefully with a Kleenex from the box on the desk and puts it in an open plastic bag. She does the same with the carton top on the night stand and the script.

When she gets back to the kitchen, the carton she has left on the counter is sitting in the red puddle of syrup spreading out across the paper towel. Cassandra takes another baggy from the bottom drawer and puts the leaky cartons in it, closes the top, and drops the baggy into her purse. Then she picks up the phone again.

The information operator on the other end is sullen. "Hold a minute for that listing," he tells her and she copies down the Gay and Lesbian Film Festival headquarters number on the back of her Visa bill envelope.

"I'm with *Windy City*," Cassandra says the name of the Chicago gay paper. "We'd like to do an interview with some black lesbian filmmakers from the festival." When she hangs up again, Cassandra knows that Ellen Gilly is staying at the Hyatt Regency on Wacker. While she waits for her cab, she rings Solange Orstrowski to see if Sally O. really wants to do her that favor.

IX

Cassandra holds her badge open beside her face in the doorway of Ellen Gilly's hotel room, while Ellen looks her up and down in the dim hall light. Under the glow of the deco wall lamp, Ellen's eyes are opaque. They give Cassandra back nothing but the glimmer of her own reflection. Behind her, the room is darker than the hall, and warmer.

"Would you mind if I come in, Ms. Gilly?" Cassandra asks. "It's getting cold out here."

"I'm sorry," Ellen Gilly is laughing awkwardly. The laughter seems wrong. Cassandra has pictured this face as naturally mournful. Ellen opens the door wide and steps away from it to let Cassandra by in a gesture that is almost welcoming.

"What can I do for you today, Detective?" A television
set in the heavy, dark wood hutch is playing reruns of
Jeopardy. Ellen Gilly points a long, complicated-looking
remote at the screen and snaps the picture off.

When the room is quiet Cassandra says, "We thought
you might want to know Lynette Devereaux is dead."

"That's nice," Ellen says. "Who's *we?*" She drops herself
in the low, padded hotel chair, seeming soft-bellied and
harmless, slouching with her legs crossed and her arms
resting open on the chair's thin wooden rests. "Is there any
special reason the Chicago Police Department is doing me
this service or were you just interested in meeting me,
Detective Hope?"

The directness catches Cassandra by surprise and what
she says next comes out in a stutter. "We know Ms.
Devereaux was a friend of yours and just thought you'd like
to know before there was an announcement." Cassandra
steadies her voice. "As a courtesy."

"A courtesy." Ellen repeats. "I see." She is drumming her
fingers on the wooden end of the arm rest slowly, the way an
old cat swings its tail, possessed of patience. "Well, that's not
like Lynette, and it's not like any Police Department I've ever
heard of." Ellen pauses as if the idea is just occurring to her.
"Maybe then courtesy is like you, Cassandra. Could that
be?"

Ellen Gilly's familiarity is making Cassandra nervous. Or
maybe the standing is making her tired, feeling vaguely like
she is having an audience with some faded monarch spread
out in a cheap upholstered hotel throne. Cassandra cannot
see Lynette with Ellen Gilly, not in a million years.

"And maybe this visit isn't so official. You and Lynette
Devereaux were lovers, weren't you? Cassandra. Cassie.
Cassie Hope." Ellen's eyes roll up as if she is inventing the
name in her mind. "When you said your name at the door
I thought it rang a bell, an old one, and I remember now."
Ellen Gilly recrosses her legs with effort and her fingers
begin to drum again peacefully on the end of the arm rest.
"I'm sorry I left you standing in the hall so long, Cassie
honey, but seeing you there was kind of a shock. I didn't
really believe they let lesbians on the police force in Chicago.
Much less made them detectives." Ellen Gilly goes on

smiling closed-mouthed, poised and asking, "How are *you*
holding up?"—not waiting for Cassandra to answer—"I've
heard a lot about you over the years. Not from Lyn, you
know, but from friends of Lyn's—mutual friends. I'd gotten
so I didn't care for Lyn. Maybe because she got everything
she ever wanted without working for it." Ellen Gilly's voice
goes sharp and ugly for a moment, before it softens again
and her face relaxes into all the worn-out shoes of faces
Cassandra remembers from growing up on in the low-rise
project on Racine Street, her mother's friends calling out in
the afternoons from their porches for Cassandra and the
other neighbor children to mind them. Ellen Gilly's voice is
tough like theirs, street-righteous and knowing. It seems to
say, *Do you think I can't see who you are, standing there
with a police badge all polly-fancy, Cassie Hope.*

Cassie, Ellen Gilly calls—not Cassandra, a name puffed
up big with plans of who she was going to be. *Cassie.*
Shortened and familiar like the older women on her block
used to say it, gently scolding her, bringing her down to size.
Her name in the mouth of this woman shrinks Cassandra
down again to where she's from, who she used to be.

"Lynette Devereaux liked to wipe her butt with people
like you and me, girls just this far from the projects." Ellen
says. "I wonder if you didn't hate her too."

"No." But Cassandra wonders if it's not true, if
somewhere behind her ambitions she doesn't hate people like
Lynette and Luther going through the world like a hot knife
through butter. "I didn't hate her," Cassandra decides.

"Well, I did," says Ellen. "So I guess that means you've
come courtesy-calling in the wrong place, dear."

"I guess so." But Cassandra is thinking, *maybe not*. She
says, "I'm sorry to trouble you, Ms. Gilly, but do you think I
could use your bathroom before I leave?"

Ellen Gilly points to a door on the right side of the room.
"In there," not bothering herself to get up. From the
bathroom Cassandra can hear that the television is playing
again, low volume.

Cassandra flips on the bathroom fan to hide the sound
of her hands in Ellen Gilly's things. She is going through
them, the bags and the satchels looking for the pills which
the *PDR* promised would be blue and D-shaped. The

intimacy of the exercise surprises her, the touching of private things, and for a moment her eyes and palms are wet. When she finds the pills in the flowered toiletry bag on the back of the toilet, she shakes one out of the bottle, hurriedly. In the mirror she watches her reflection drop it into the deep patch pocket of her blazer. There are syringes too, in the bag with the pills. Cassandra leaves them, but she puts the drinking glass by sink in her pocket in case there are prints to match those on the juice cartons. Cassandra reads the prescription date on the bottle before she puts it away again. It was filled two weeks before with a hundred tablets. The label at the bottom says two more refills. She flushes the toilet and runs some more water in the sink. Afterwards she walks out into the room with a hand in her pocket to hide the bulge of the glass.

"Thank you for your time, Ms. Gilly. We'll stay in touch," Cassandra says.

At seven-thirty, the Medical Examiner's Office is cleared out, but Solange is there, still smoking in her cubicle. It takes Solange an hour to test the cartons of Queen Bee juice. She says Diabinese is the blue pill and is in one out of three of the cartons of Queen Bee juice. There are traces in the empty carton from the trash in the guest room and in the sticky red stain on the script. There are no clear prints on the containers but Lynette's and Cassandra's. Still, hunched over with her eye butted up against the lens of Solange's microscope, the pinhole leaks in the tops of the cartons look to Cassandra big enough for a truck convoy to drive through. Not enough to take to the State's Attorney without the physical evidence. But it's a start. It takes Lynette's death out of the category of accident, and that at least lets Cassandra tell herself she's doing something about it.

"You feel so tense." Solange is standing behind her, hands massaging Cassandra's neck, her breasts pressed against Cassandra's back. "How about that drink?" Sal offers. "How about we bring back old times?" Her hands slide warm down Cassandra's arms and back up again, feeling hot even through the woolen sleeves of her pullover, the cranberry cashmere Luther gave her last Christmas. Sometimes Cassandra would like to make it work with

Luther for real. But old times, she'd like them back too. Sometimes Cassandra feels like there is a spring inside her hips that's wound so tight it's about to pop. But old times are gone. They are dead along with Lynette Devereaux.

"Maybe a raincheck." Cassandra stands, turning.

She watches Solange's body go slack, shoulders slumping as she steps away from Cassandra. Solange picks up the test results from the desk and hands the paper over, all business again. "Your copy."

Slipping the paper into her bag, Cassandra says, "I'll call you," but they both know what that means.

"Whatever." Solange is rapping a fresh pack of cigarettes on the side of the lab bench, watching her as she stands in the doorway. "Don't do me any favors, Cassie." But Cassandra can feel her eyes all the way down the empty hall.

◆

At nine-thirty, Luther is already in bed at home with his reading glasses on. Luther pulls the heavy tortoise-shell frames off by the temples and sets them on the nightstand beside his book. "Where were you?" he says as if he's missed her.

"Here and there," Cassandra tells him. Lowering herself to her side of the bed, she asks, "Had a long day?"

Luther groans. "You look better." Sitting up, he folds his arms around her, sighing.

"I feel better." Cassandra tells him, "The doctors say it was no big deal. Too much stress, not enough sleep." She lies to him, laughing. "They put me on vitamins."

"Vitamin E?" Luther pulls her over with him as he falls back onto the bed. His hands massage familiar circles on her ass. She pretends not to notice. They are both laughing now, expectantly, so close she can feel the heat from his open mouth. "That vitamin E thing is just for men."

As he rolls on top of her, Luther says, "Before you make me forget, there was a call on the machine from someone named Ellen Gilly."

The name stops Cassandra from grinding her hips under Luther's.

Luther stops too and she can feel his anger. "What's wrong?"

Cassandra kisses him quickly, a close-mouth smack. "It's just some work. But I've got to go," she says still laughing, sliding out from under him to call Ellen Gilly on the kitchen phone. "But Luther honey, hold that thought."

♦

Glancing up at the clock on the microwave, Cassandra calls a cab. When she hangs up the phone, Luther is listening from the doorway, arms crossed. He catches Cassandra by the hand and laces his fingers in hers as she brushes past him, keeping hold of her hand until his arm is stretched full length. "Come back to bed," Luther says.

"I can't help it that I have to work." Cassandra scoops up her clothes in a pile, the sweater and slacks from their ball on the chair, her blazer from the doorknob. She takes them with her to the bathroom, stopping on the way at the little closet in the hall where she keeps a small recorder and microphone.

"Cassandra?" Luther is knocking on the bathroom door. "What's going on?"

Cassandra drops the recorder into her blazer pocket as she opens the bathroom door. "I'm going out," she says.

"Yeah, I can see that." Luther is standing with a hand on either side of the door frame. "Some woman calls here. You get up out of the bed and go running off to see her at ten o'clock at night." As Cassandra ducks quickly under his arm, he catches her again by the wrist. "Cassie, don't you try to make a fool out of me." He has her tight enough to twist her arm, but it's Luther who looks as if he wants to cry.

Outside there is the single blast of a car horn.

"My cab is here." When he finally lets her go, Cassandra has to run to catch it.

"I'll see you when I get back," she tells him from the doorway. Grunting, Luther sinks down onto the couch, throwing his feet up over the edge. As Cassandra shuts the door she can hear him shouting after her, "You be sure to give your girlfriend my love."

♦

Luther is still on the couch when Cassandra gets home, but he's sitting up, cracking Brazil nuts into the big ceramic bowl. There's a bottle of Glenfiddich on the coffeetable that wasn't there before and half a glass of scotch making wet rings on the glass top.

"How's your girlfriend?" he hisses, but Cassandra walks right past to the bathroom and locks the door without looking back.

She steps out of her slacks and sits down on the toilet, remembering Ellen Gilly's dark little box of a hotel room. Cassandra can see it all over again when she presses the play button on her recorder and the tape in her pocket begins to roll, giving a soundtrack to the pictures in her mind.

INT   **HYATT REGENCY**   **NIGHT**

Through the open shades, the city is twinkling out over her balcony: the Chicago river and the big clock on the top of the Wrigley Building. ELLEN GILLY is facing CASSANDRA at the open door. As Cassandra steps through it, Ellen crosses to the table by the mini-bar and pours herself a glass of wine from a split of white with a screw-off top.

ELLEN GILLY (Raising her wine glass.) I'd offer you some but I know you can't stay. (Emphatically.) Detective Hope, you took one of my pills and I'd like it back. You see, I don't have many and I'm going to need it for the train ride home.

CASSANDRA Did you know Lynette Devereaux was probably killed with the same drug? Diabinese.

ELLEN GILLY You don't say. May I have my pill back?

CASSANDRA Lynette Devereaux didn't slip in the shower—she got punchy and fell. Hypoglycemic they call it. On diabetes medicine.

ELLEN GILLY That's a very interesting coincidence.

CASSANDRA Maybe it is and maybe it isn't. It isn't if somebody drugged Lynette Devereaux's Queen Bee juice. Maybe they meant for her to fall into a coma, maybe die in her sleep, but she passed out in the shower instead, my shower. All the better because now it looks like an accident—to everybody but me.

ELLEN GILLY   (Smiling.)   An interesting idea but I don't know how you're ever going to prove it.

CASSANDRA   That's for the State's Attorney. I only need to convince myself. Are you a diabetic, Ms. Gilly? Diabinese is a drug for late-onset diabetes.

ELLEN GILLY   (Testily.)   I know what it is. I could have told you I was on Diabinese without putting you to so much trouble, Detective Hope. There's no crime in that. I've had a prescription for years.

CASSANDRA   The prescription for the bottle in your bag was refilled two weeks ago. I wonder why you're down to only four pills in two weeks?

ELLEN GILLY   The train ride. I spilled them in the bathroom on the train. The floor was filthy, so I threw them out. There were six left. I took two— you took one.

CASSANDRA   Funny that so much Diabinese turned up in the Queen Bee juice from Lynette's overnight bag. Did you know Lynette always bought strawberry flavor? The juice in her bag was raspberry. She thought it tasted funny. Funny thing if you were on the same train. Not much trouble to verify, but I already know because Lynette told me you had threatened her the night she died. She was afraid you might hurt her, Ellen. What if she was right? What if you were watching and waiting for Lynette to go to sleep, maybe go to the ladies' room, and then it would only take a minute to switch Lynette's juice for the juice you bought and doctored. Maybe you pretended to go to the ladies' room yourself, and on the way back you sat down accidentally-on-purpose in Lynette's seat. Who would notice? What you didn't count on was drugging me.

ELLEN GILLY   I didn't drug you.

CASSANDRA   Somebody did. And you'll understand if I'm taking it personally.

ELLEN GILLY   I don't know what you're talking about. Diabinese comes in little blue pills.

CASSANDRA Which the *PDR* says are soluble in alcohol. Not much trouble to grind them up into powder. Somebody dissolved them and shot the drug through the tops of the plastic caps with a syringe. Did you know there's a stain at the bottom of Lynette's overnight bag from a leaky bottle? And I believe there are syringes in your bag.

ELLEN GILLY I'm a diabetic. I have a prescription for the syringes, the same as I have a prescription for the Diabinese. And I don't see why any of this speculation should involve me.

CASSANDRA Lynette did. She wrote your initials on the glass in my shower when she realized she was dying. It was the last thing she did. I know about her review of your film. I know you fought with Lynette. I know how much you hated her, because you told me that part yourself last time I was here.

ELLEN GILLY You can't prove any of this. (Slowly, gaining confidence, speaking almost to herself.) If you could, you'd have come here to arrest me. And you haven't, have you? Everybody knows about the review Lynette did of *Culture Shock*. It was spite and jealousy. Everybody knew she was a mean-spirited bitch, and I'm not the only person she used. That's a big club. Maybe you just need to pin her death on someone, so you don't have to take the guilt, dear. What do they say? Wishes are flesh. And how many times have you wished it, Cassie, that you were she, that she was gone. And for that now you want to tar me. (Slyly.) Goodness, who's to say that there aren't bottles of drug-laced Queen Bee all over Philadelphia? Think of that, Detective.

CASSANDRA Is that a threat?

ELLEN GILLY Oh, I don't make threats—you do. I just don't understand a thing you're talking about. But I'm just saying suppose for a minute that maybe this is another tragic case of product tampering. Then who's to blame?

CASSANDRA You know I could make trouble for you.

ELLEN GILLY   And I could make trouble for you too,
Cassie Hope. I know who you are underneath that
badge and the fresh coat of paint. I know who you
are and who you want to be. Remember that.
Remember I could make trouble for a lot of people.
(She stops as if she is going to say more but instead lets out an
audible breath.)   We're not so different, Cassie Hope. I
could give you good advice, let sleeping dogs—   (She
stops and smiles again; her voice is almost serene.)   Can you
find your way out Detective? I don't think we have
anything else to talk about. I'll be going back home
on the early train tomorrow morning, unless you can
think of a good reason I need to stay.

There is nothing else after that but the sound of the
closing door and Cassandra's own footsteps in the hall.
Cassandra clicks off the tape, feeling sick to her stomach.
She can guess what Ellen Gilly is going to do when she goes
back to Philadelphia, what Cassandra would do in Ellen
Gilly's position—poison enough Queen Bee juice to muddy
the waters. But there isn't near enough evidence to charge
her. Not enough even to be sure she killed Lynette. No
prints, no physical evidence to link Ellen Gilly to the
tampered juice, and a lot of diabetics out there in the world.
A lot of hate. Against not even enough evidence to be sure
that Cassandra isn't just making it all up—a suspect and a
murder make herself a hero. To make up for Lynette's death,
or for who Cassandra is—for being alive—for the times she
has looked at women like Lynette on the street and wanted
to kill them herself.

Cassandra hangs her blazer on the bathroom hook by
her robe and turns on the shower, thinking if Ellen Gilly
killed Lynette maybe she's already spiked all Queen Bee juice
in Philadelphia to cover herself. Thinking none of it will
bring Lynette back. Cassandra is wondering if that's what
she really wants—Lynette alive, because Lynette is so much
easier to take as a memory. Maybe that means everything
Ellen Gilly said was true, about Cassandra. About Lynette?

Cassandra steps onto the plastic mat on the floor of the
shower, raising her face to meet the spray. Water splatters
over her chest. It winds in ribbons down her legs, washing

into the shiny, metal spokes of the drain, washing her tears away as if they were never there at all.

Outside Cassandra can hear Luther's voice calling, asking her what she thinks she's doing. As the water washes over her face, she closes her eyes and lets him go on calling.

A SPECIAL EDUCATION

J. D. Shaw

Boston has become a city of young people. There are too many colleges, and too many of the kids stay there after graduation. Not that I meet many of those types. My job deals with a different element. In homicide we don't always get to talk to people who wash themselves a lot.

My name is Harry Hutchinson. I've been a police detective for six years now. And once, last winter, I did get to deal with the clean-cut ones.

It was a little before midnight, windy, sleety as December here can be, and I was looking for an address on Beacon Street. It wasn't the part of Beacon that the tourists ever see, but it wasn't a bad area either, several blocks of nice old ivy-covered townhouses that had been divided up into apartments.

My address, 361, was in the middle of the block. It was a nice double-doored job. There was a uniformed officer standing in front and I showed him my credentials. I walked into a red carpeted lobby. There was a wide staircase with a beautiful dark wood banister and the same red carpet. On either side of the staircase were nice-looking, dark wood doors leading to, I'm sure, nice apartments.

I climbed the stairs. The second floor matched the first and the third was another match. However, the apartment I was seeking was on the fourth floor, and there didn't seem to be a fourth floor. There was an extra door up here, stuck in the corner. I opened it and saw more stairs, not carpeted, very narrow and turned at odd angles.

At the top I entered a not-very-attractive door and found myself in the confusion that always accompanies murder. The medical men and the photographer and the police stepping over each other. I called my hellos.

"She's over here," said one of the uniforms.

The apartment had what looked like two living rooms. I walked through the first one and into the second. There was a big chandelier, so I supposed it had been a dining room at one time, but it was bigger than the other one, with a nice fireplace, still smoldering. My quick observation of the place said young, attic treasures, maybe a year away from student days. Everything was a bit frazzled except a wall of very good and very expensive stereo equipment. The posters on the walls were framed, and there was one Ansel Adams print. There was definitely no plan and no color scheme. I could almost picture the occupants. Female, because of all the pastel colors and a few touches like curtains; active, because of the general disorder; beginning careers, because of a tossed briefcase and computer and sheets and sheets of paper on the table; not committed to calling this a real home, because, somehow, it wasn't.

The young woman lying in the futon didn't fit the picture. She was sprawled face up in a mess of blood. She had been shot more than once in the head and that produced a gore you never get used to seeing.

She was slim and dressed in jeans and a sweatshirt. She must have had beautiful hair; what you could see of it was shiny and black and full and long.

No matter how often I come to a scene like this, I always feel the bile rise in my throat and I always feel a few seconds of real physical rage. I must stand very still and let it pass. It does. The rage becomes a tenseness that doesn't go away until I find the answers.

"Her name is Christine Jamison," one of the uniformed cops told me. He showed me a snapshot of her. She had been beautiful and terribly young. "Who found the body?" I asked.

"One of the girls living here. There are three of them all together. She's in the first bedroom there." The uniformed cop pointed me through the other living room and down a narrow hallway.

I decided go talk to the girl while the scientific types did their thing.

I knocked and opened the door at the same time. Murder doesn't blend with manners.

A large-boned girl, strikingly lovely, sat on the bed, hugging her knees to her chest.

She unwrapped herself at my introduction, stood and reached out her hand.

"Barbara Burnes," she offered. She had brown hair, cut no-nonsense, at chin length, brown eyes, and a face that was blotchy with tears. But her youth and bone structure and fine skin held up. At her worst, she beat the average. Her voice was low and controlled.

She answered my questions quickly, looking me straight in the eye while she talked. She worked, she told me, in a bank as a credit analyst in the lending department. She had come home a little before six o'clock and had had to eat her salad standing up at the sink. Christine didn't join her, wouldn't even move her papers so that Barbara could sit down. She had then gone out to a movie with a friend and out for coffee afterward. She had returned home at about 11:30.

"What were Christine's plans for the evening?" I asked.

"None. She had work to do. Christine didn't go out much anymore. She was really bogged down at her office. She had a big report due." There was a touch of disapproval in her voice.

"I asked her to go to the movie with me, but I wasn't surprised when she said no."

She told me that Christine had been a media planner for an advertising firm. She was up for a big promotion and she worked all the time.

"Did you get along?" I asked her.

"Of course. We all went to school together, Christine, Betsy, and me. We've known each other forever."

"And you've lived here how long?"

"We signed a two-year lease. It will be up in two months."

She went on to tell me how close they were, what good friends, and so on. She said too much. I've never known anyone who lived together that didn't have a few little shady places. I kept pushing.

Finally, with a sigh she admitted that both of the girls got on her nerves sometimes. "Actually, everyone gets on my nerves sooner or later," she said.

I agreed with that point of view but asked for specifics.

"She just wasn't much fun anymore. She was so driven, like a workaholic. I would have been surprised if she had stayed with us when our lease was up. She was very impatient with us having parties and having people over."

I pushed some more and Barbara finally erupted.

"Okay, okay. We weren't close anymore, not at all. She was so single-minded, so superior. I missed the Christine I used to know." There was real anger there. And loss. She sounded like people do when they've been left behind.

Just then the door opened and I was motioned outside by the uniformed cop.

"The other roommate is coming up the stairs with her boyfriend," he said.

I met them at the door and directed them away from the scene in the second living room into the narrow hallway and explained what had happened.

The small, blond frail-looking woman who was watching me with big Goldie Hawn eyes almost collapsed at the news. The young man with her put a protective arm around her and we all went into the bedroom where Barbara Burnes was still standing by the bed. The two girls hugged each other. The new one, whose name I found out was Betsy Orbaugh, was sobbing with breath-catching heaves.

Barbara sat her down on the bed, and the young man, who introduced himself as Greg Martin, sat down with her and again put his arm around her.

It's only been in the past year or so that everyone has started to look like teenagers to me. Greg was in his early twenties, as were the others. So that only makes them fifteen years younger than me. But I don't remember looking that young when I was twelve. He had a round, pleasant face that should have been grinning. He was not comfortable with grief.

"So," I said to the two on the bed, "Where have you been this evening?"

Greg carefully removed his arm from around Betsy as though afraid she would somehow disintegrate without it. He stood up.

This was a very small room, only about five feet of floor space. Greg was pacing every square inch.

"We met at a bar after work with some people, went out for Italian and then to another bar afterward, like we do every Thursday night," Greg told me impatiently.

I took out a pad of paper and tore off three sheets and handed them each one.

"Write down the times and places of where you were this evening," I told them.

Barbara and Greg found pens and started writing. Betsy sat looking at her piece of paper, her face crumpled with tears.

Greg sat down beside her again, the trusty arm ready. "We were together all evening, Lieutenant. Can't I just do it for both of us?"

"No, I'm afraid not," I said.

I turned to Betsy. "I know it's difficult, but try. You were together all evening?"

She opened her mouth to reply, but Greg said quickly, "I told you we were." People who answer for other people really irk me.

"Miss Orbaugh, when did you last see Christine?" I asked Betsy directly.

"Not since she left for work this morning," Greg said, "and really, officer, can't you see she's upset?"

This wasn't going to work. "You stay here, and take your time, but please write down what I asked for," I said to Betsy. "You two come with me."

It was convenient that there were three bedrooms. I put Barbara and Greg in the other two. I didn't want them comparing notes about the time frame. I generally like to see witnesses together for a few minutes. Questions and answers are the bones of my business, but it is in the nuances of relationships where you start to see below the surface.

I went back out to the murder room. The experts were finishing up.

"About how long?" I asked the doctor. They hate that question. It's a stupid one, but we always ask. It's only the medical examiners in Agatha Christie and Ellery Queen that can come up with exact times of death. We've lost something with our new techniques. There are a million variables.

"Somewhere over four hours," the doctor said. Which meant that rigor mortis had begun and that was all I was going to get out of him.

After the body was removed, I had Betsy and Barbara come out and look around. Nothing was missing. This was not robbery, not on the fourth floor, the worst apartment, and a wall full of stereo equipment sitting there untapped.

Everyone had their hands tested for powder residue. Not that that is any indication of anything since the invention of gloves.

Then we got lucky. I don't much count on luck, and I don't trust it very much. But sometimes it's there. This time it showed up twice.

Barbara told me she had left for the movie at 6:45. And Mrs. Mitchell, third-floor resident, had seen her go. Mrs. Mitchell had been waiting in the lobby for her nephew to pick her up. It turned out that the nephew was late and she had been at that window watching for him so he wouldn't have to park. She had stood there from 6:40 until 7:20, when he finally showed up. Nobody came in the building during that time. Our first piece of luck.

Our second was the answering machine. There was a message on it recorded at 7:10. It was for Christine, a guy working with her on the project who had the figures she wanted. He asked her to call back within fifteen minutes because he was leaving the office then. The guy wanted to know where was she anyway? If he was working his tail off for her, why wasn't she there to get the figures?

Okay, just like Ellery Queen, we had the time of death. After 6:45 when Barbara left and before 7:10. You don't often get this lucky this fast.

Unless, of course, Barbara did it before she left. We had established what weapon was used. Christine's father had insisted they have a gun for protection. That gun had been placed neatly back on the shelf behind the stereo. It had been fired recently. We were sure that tests would prove that it was the murder weapon; the bullet that missed, the one that embedded itself in the wall, was the same caliber. However, the gun would have a big cross section of fingerprints on it. All three women had loved showing it to people. According to Betsy and Barbara, it had sat out, in plain sight, on that shelf behind the stereo.

◆

It was time to interview everybody individually.

Barbara didn't have much more to add to what she had already told me. She had such a straightforward attitude, looking you directly in the eye, with that controlled voice. I liked her. I hoped she hadn't killed Christine.

"I was the last person to see her alive," she said a couple of times.

"Were you? I'd say that the killer was the last person to see her alive," I said.

She got my meaning real quick and gave me another of those direct looks. I questioned her about the gun.

"Christine's father told us to keep it loaded, but nobody knew it was loaded except the three of us."

"Christine's father doesn't read statistics," I said. "A handy gun can make a robbery into a murder, but robbers don't usually bother to put the gun back on a shelf."

I asked her if there was any friction between Betsy and Christine.

She shook her head and looked at me, tried a small smile. "Betsy is, well, Betsy. She doesn't get angry, she just gets hurt."

I asked her to tell me about Greg Martin.

"What about him? He and Betsy have been dating for almost a year. Betsy adores him. He's a nice enough guy, a little on the know-it-all side. Not my type."

And I came to agree. Greg Martin was someone I liked less and less the more I talked to him. Real quick he wanted me to know he had graduated from Harvard. Now, understand, in some kind of perverse way everyone who lives in Boston is inordinately proud of that fine institution of learning, even if we didn't go there ourselves. But I'd met the type before, those who wanted to establish, within six seconds of introduction, that they had gone there. Invariably the high point of their lives had been that acceptance letter. Nothing they had done in school or since quite lived up to it. Almost as quickly, Greg wanted me to know that the girls had all attended a state university. It was information I didn't need to know.

Greg worked at the same advertising firm as Christine, had been there for four years. He was grateful that she had introduced him to Betsy. He didn't seem to have a great deal of admiration for Christine's abilities at work. He kept referring back to that state school.

"But wasn't she up for some big promotion?" I asked.

Greg was a person who was comfortable in action. He had sat down and stood up several times during our interview, and when I asked this question he stood up again.

"She was dreaming. Had the idea that all this extra work was going to do it for her. Well, let me tell you, it doesn't work like that. She refused to play office politics. I tried to guide her about that, but she wouldn't listen."

He sat again, with finality.

I looked at the paper he had given me.

"You met Betsy a little after 7:30. Where were you before that?" I asked him.

"I played racquetball with one of the vice presidents. That can't do any harm, huh?" He looked very pleased with himself. "We finished about six thirty. Then I picked up some cleaning and ran home to change. It's a Thursday night routine."

"You never come here to pick Betsy up?"

"No, not on Thursday nights. She goes out with some of her artist friends for a drink and then she meets me at the bar. There were about eight of us tonight. I wrote down all the names for you." He pointed to the paper I was still holding.

We were sitting in the first living room. Greg kept looking toward the other room. But that wasn't surprising. We all have a bit of ghoulish curiosity.

I asked him what he thought of Barbara.

"Oh, she's okay. She can be very sarcastic. She's pretty cool about everything. She sure isn't my type, a little too sure of herself, if you know what I mean. And, detective, I might add, she does have a terrible temper."

Without Greg around, Betsy could talk just fine. She had calmed down. Her pale skin hadn't recovered from the tears as well as Barbara's. But she was making a valiant effort to get it together.

"Where do you work?" I asked her.

"I'm a graphic artist for a company that makes tee shirts and mugs, that sort of stuff," she pointed to the sweatshirt she was wearing. It had a picture of a cross-eyed pigeon about to dump on a man's head and the caption, "Look Up—See Your Horizons."

"From the time you left work, tell me where you were," I asked her.

Her story jibed with Greg's. It was a Thursday night routine.

"You were with your artist friends from 5:30 until 7:30?" I asked her.

"Well, I don't know exactly. I didn't look at a clock and I don't wear a watch. After I left them I stopped in a couple of stores walking to meet Greg. It was very cold outside. It's about a mile walk."

"And Greg was there when you got there?"

She paused. "I don't exactly remember. I think he was." She kept twisting a strand of her rather wispy blond hair. "I get it mixed up with all the other times, but I think he was."

I could accept Betsy on that level. She looked to me like she floated along just a little left of reality. Her appeal was on a little girl level and she could carry off her flightiness. On her it was cute. But it was not helpful in a murder investigation.

"How did you get along with Christine?"

"Oh great. We've known each other such a long time. She was my freshman roommate you know." I could see her starting to fall apart again. I quickly went on.

"But now, here, you all got along?"

"Sure. She was awfully busy all the time. She was impatient with Barbara and me. But that was just because of the pressure she was under at work and all." She thought for a moment. "Barbara gets a little impatient with me sometimes too."

There were shadows here, lots of them. These three girls were feeling some strains of living together.

I asked Betsy about the gun. "You knew the gun was loaded. What about Greg? Did he know?"

"I guess so," she said. "He's always around here. I think he probably knew."

I asked Betsy about what kind of working relationship Christine and Greg had.

"Well, Greg said that Christine wasn't going to get that big promotion. No way, Greg said. It will probably be someone who's been there a while. I mean, Christine's only been there a year. I mean, look at Greg, he's real buddy-buddy with all the top guys and he really knows what's going on. He was worried about Christine, about her being disappointed. He asked me to talk to her about not setting herself up for such a big let down."

I let the three of them settle into one of the bedrooms for a while. I walked into the murder room and stood there, absorbing the atmosphere. It was time to start putting it all together. I didn't like the way it was adding up. Barbara, Betsy, and Greg, none of them had absolute alibis for the time of the murder. But Mrs. Mitchell would have seen anyone come in the door. That pointed only to Barbara. She had a temper. Who else could it possibly be? She was cool enough to try to pull off something like this. It didn't make sense to me, but then murder never does.

The one other idea was another occupant of the building, already in. We investigated each apartment. We came up empty. Six other apartments, two away on vacation, Mrs. Mitchell accounted for, a couple living on the first floor where Mrs. Mitchell would have seen them going upstairs, another couple who were out for the evening, and one other woman, age seventy-three, legally blind.

We were back to Barbara again. It all pointed to her. But somehow I didn't want to take her down to the station for more questioning, not yet.

I had Barbara and Betsy call and arrange to stay with friends, and I had them gather up some clothes to take with them. This apartment would be sealed. We would drive the women where they were going and Greg home. That would about wrap it up for tonight.

But I hated to leave it. Everything they say about the trail growing cold in forty-eight hours is true. Gossip becomes fact and fact becomes illusion. I resented the need for sleep for myself and for others.

I didn't see Greg. So I looked around. His curiosity had gotten the better of him. He was standing in the second living room.

"What a terrible thing," he said. The futon had been taken apart and the covering had gone to the lab along with many other items, but there were stains everywhere. They'd be there for a long time. I doubted the floorboards would ever come clean.

Betsy came and stood in the doorway. She didn't look toward where the futon had been.

"Let's go, I can't stand this," she said and I could see her shiver.

Greg went over to her and put the ever faithful arm around her.

"It's cold in here," she said.

Greg looked at her with that superior air I found so irritating. "Well, don't get dramatic and go into the death and cold thing. I've told you a dozen times that your fireplace is too near the thermostat. When you have a fire, it makes the whole place cold. You should have it moved to the other room." He smiled at her patronizingly.

I looked into the fireplace. It was dead, cold. How did he know there had been a fire smoldering when I had arrived and probably blazing earlier than that?

When he looked at me, for reaffirmation of his clever suggestion, he saw my face and realized his mistake.

He deflated, just sank in on himself, like a sock without a foot or a glove without a hand.

Greg and I sat in that cold room the rest of the night. Once started, he couldn't get the words out fast enough. He could not have lived with his crime, not really, not on any level acceptable to himself. I could see that.

He had not meant to hurt her. When the man he had played racquetball with had told him that Christine was getting the promotion and that, in essence, Greg would be working for her, he had been so angry, so incensed, that he had rushed over to the apartment and had yelled and screamed at her.

"How could this happen?" he had asked. "I'm better than you. My God, I went to Harvard."

Finally, he had cried. On a different level, to be sure, but somehow, for him, that was almost as big a crime as murder. Christine had been sympathetic. When they heard Barbara coming up the stairs, she had told him to wait in Betsy's bedroom until he could pull himself together.

But he hadn't.

After Barbara left, he was going to go, was about to walk out the door, but he picked up the gun and said, "Why don't you just go ahead and shoot me. You might as well."

He didn't remember pulling the trigger. It hadn't seemed possible that she had fallen, bloody, down into the futon. And then all he could do was try to pretend it hadn't happened. He had waited on the stairs until Mrs. Mitchell left.

When he finished telling me everything, he looked at me earnestly.

"It doesn't make sense," he said quietly. "I did all the right things. I had the right credentials, the right school, the right networking. I spent time with the right people, played racquetball with the V.P.s, took clients to my club. And she sat in her office with her head stuck in her reports. She didn't know how to act, how could she? She went to that cow college and on a scholarship, no less. It just doesn't make sense."

People who commit crimes are people who are flawed. Mostly they're just stupid, or they're people who are missing some control lever that the rest of us have, or they're people whose sense of priorities is way out of kilter. And, as far as I'm concerned, they're all insane at the moment they commit the crime. Temporary insanity is the reason a crime is committed, not the reason a person should be found not guilty.

There is a fine line between accident and intent. That is for the courts to deal with. But a lovely young woman had been killed. That demanded justice.

When they took Greg away, in handcuffs, he kept shaking his head like he didn't understand. I don't think he did. There are some things even a Harvard education won't prepare you for.

Rose Fever

G. V. Babish

Fred stepped onto his deck after breakfast, checked that the weather was as fine as the early broadcast had promised, and then saw that dog.

That dog was digging in his roses. Again! Fred had told Willis and told Willis to keep that dog on a leash, but Willis said the dog liked to roam a bit. Fred took a stone and aimed it at the dog's back. A high yelp let Fred know his aim was good. It let Willis know too.

"You leave my dog alone," an angry voice came from next door, and Fred saw his neighbor, Willis, stomping across the grass.

"Don't come into my yard," Fred stomped himself down his three steps and toward the border of their property. "That mangy mongrel has been digging in my rose border. I put new Queen Elizabeth roses in yesterday and your dog uprooted two of them."

"It's too late to put in rose bushes," Willis glared at Fred. "If they die, it's your own stupid fault." Rex, that mongrel, dug energetically at another bush.

Fred pushed the dog away from the bush and Willis pushed Fred. Fred raised his hand and noticed Mary walking toward him and Willis. Abashed, Fred glared at the dog.

"Willis," said Mary, "it's time to get ready for the dentist. Good morning, Fred." She turned serenely, hooked her hand in Rex's collar and led him back to the house.

Willis glared at Fred. "Your roses are getting aphids," he said spitefully as he followed Mary.

Fred went to his tool shed and banged the doors. He felt better but he still wanted to hit something. Rummaging a bit, he brought out the old wheelbarrow, an iron rake, and a cardboard box. He went in the house and saw that Louise was loading the washer.

"I'm going to dig out the poison ivy," Fred announced belligerently.

Louise nodded calmly. After forty-three years of marriage, she knew when to comment and when not to.

Fred changed into a really old shirt, trousers, and work shoes with steel toes and put a mask on his face. He picked up gardening gloves. He worked hard for an hour, grubbing into the hedge at the back where the poison ivy had really taken hold. He chopped it with the rake, clipped it into bits and stuffed the bits into the box. Sweat poured down his face. He pretended it was Willis's face when he swung the rake. "Take that," he thought. He chopped at the ivy. "Tell me when to plant roses, will you. Which roses won the prize last year? Was it your Willis Wonder? No. It was Fred's Fantasy! I know how to care for roses." Chop. Chop.

When the box was full of ivy clippings, Fred stopped. He put all the tools on the wheelbarrow and headed for the shed, still sweating. Putting the rake away and taking out the mulcher, he mulched all the ivy clippings into a trash bag. Then he drew off the gloves, carefully turning them inside out and never touching the outside. He walked to the house where Louise opened the door for him. He dropped the gloves into the laundry tub. Carefully he put on another pair of gardening gloves and then undressed completely. He put all the clothes in the washer including the two pairs of gloves and set the shoes on newspaper.

"I'll clean the shoes after my shower," he told his wife.

"Okay, then I'll wash these things later."

That evening, when Louise turned the TV on to watch *Jeopardy*, Fred headed for the cellar. Louise looked up, but before she asked, Fred told her, "I'm going to cut the shelves

you wanted for the linen closet. I'll close the cellar door so
the noise won't interfere with your show."

Fred took the ivy mulch into the cellar and ground it into
a fine powder. He wore a mask and an old robe of Louise's
that he sometimes used for a coverup. When he had a full
bag of poison ivy dust, he returned the trash bag of mulch to
the toolshed. Fred put the robe and mask into a trash bag
and went up to bed. First he took another shower.

The next morning Fred took the bag of ivy dust and
labeled it "Miracle Rose Powder." Then he hurried out to
the rose border. He took out his trowel and his clippers,
adjusted his hat, propped the bag of "Miracle Rose Powder"
on the edge of the rose bushes and fussed around kicking at
the bushes Rex had uprooted the day before.

Louise walked onto the deck and called him. "Come into
the house please, Fred." She was polite, but commanding.

Fred dawdled and called back, "I'm putting this new
rose powder around. Can't it wait?"

Louise was insistent. "Come in now." She pointed
accusingly at his breakfast plate and the small red pill
pushed under the place mat. "How could you forget your
blood pressure pill? It's so important for you."

Fred swallowed the pill docilely. "Maybe I'm tired. I'll
rest a bit and finish the roses later."

"Well, Mary and I are going to have our hair done."
Louise looked at him. "Can you and Willis be civil for a few
hours?"

Fred nodded and didn't look at her.

After the car drove off, Fred went into the bedroom and
peered out from behind the curtains, being careful not to let
them move. Soon, Rex went scampering out the back door
in the next yard. Fred ground his teeth but stayed in place. A
few minutes later, Willis strolled into the back yard. He was
tossing a ball, whistling and edging toward Fred's roses. Fred
kept still and watched intently.

Willis took the ball and threw it for the dog. Rex
brought it back. Willis looked at Fred's house and yard.
Then Willis threw the ball into the rose border and Rex
plunged after it. Fred beat his fist on the bedroom wall but
didn't call out.

Willis jogged over to the roses and again looked carefully all over Fred's yard. When Fred didn't appear, Willis bent down to read the bag. He grabbed it up and rushed into his house. Ten minutes later he was back with the bag and replaced it along the border. Fred smiled to himself; he noticed the bag was much smaller. He smiled even more broadly when he saw Willis in shorts and a T-shirt spraying the "Miracle Rose Powder" at the far side of his yard.

Louise came home well after lunch. Fred kissed her and complimented her on the new hairstyle. He apologized for being grumpy the past two days.

"Let's go out to dinner and see that movie you've been talking about."

Fred and Louise arrived home at 9:30 to see flashing lights from an ambulance at Willis's. Mary was getting into the ambulance, crying and looking stunned. Fred watched stoically. Willis died during the night. The doctor said it was acute respiratory distress.

After the funeral, Louise invited Mary to visit, but Mary said her married daughter had asked her to go to Connecticut. She would enjoy the visit and her grandchildren would enjoy playing with Rex.

Fred said he would mind her house until she got back. He would cut the lawn and water the flowers.

The day after Mary left, Fred cared for his roses, enjoying the quiet. He had a box of rose dust and sprayed peacefully until Louise came out to keep him company.

"I'm going to do the grocery shopping now. Do you want to go to the garden center?" Louise asked.

"No. I thought I was out of rose dust but then I found this." Fred held up the box he was using to fill the duster.

Louise glanced at the box. "Oh, yes. I filled that from the bag Mary gave me yesterday, since Willis won't be using it anymore."

THE CONFECTIONER

Meredith Suzanne Baird

Willie Pardo always knew he would have to commit suicide—he just hadn't expected it to be so soon. He was only twenty-eight and really had hoped he would make it to his thirtieth birthday. But then, he thought, this is what happens when you don't have a reason to live.

Willie wasn't merely fat—he was huge. His three chins piled on his chest and pushed up his cheeks, making his eyes appear closed even when they were wide open. The dark crop of ridiculously unruly curls growing on top of all that adiposity looked like a cheap wig. His knees, long lost to the relentless layering of blubber, would barely bend. The sight of Willie crammed into clothing that could never hope to fit was too much for most people. Stifled bursts of laughter followed him wherever he went.

He always took jobs that kept him hidden from the public. Chemical factory janitor, night watchman, airport restroom attendant. Night jobs were the best. He felt safer in the dark. It was as if the shadows made him thinner and less vulnerable. He never had a job for very long. The excuses for firing him were vague or sometimes even creative, but the real reason was always the same. He was just too fat to keep around.

He was currently working as a fry cook at a greasy spoon, but that was tenuous at best. Roy had threatened to fire him if he didn't stop eating on the job. Willie had blurred out most of what Roy had to say, but the words "slopping hogs" kept slamming through his brain.

It had been like this for years. Dr. Barnes estimated Willie's weight was on the wrong—the very wrong—side of five hundred pounds. He'd hounded him unmercifully to go on a diet. No fats, no starches, no sugar. No thanks, Willie had thought and kept on eating.

It was over now. Willie had diabetes. His pancreas—that faithful organ that had partnered Willie in his consumption of gargantuan amounts of sugar—had finally quit. He had to go on a restrictive diet, start insulin shots, change his whole lifestyle. It was all so simple to the doctor. Stop eating or die.

It was even simpler to Willie. Stop eating—and die.

So what did he have to live for? He had no friends and his family was long gone. His father had deserted them when Willie was five years old. That's when his mother stopped eating and started stuffing him. His life began to revolve around food. Finally, any activity—school, sleeping, breathing—turned into an interruption of his main purpose in life. Eating. Until now, it had been the one thing that never let Willie down.

His mother died four years earlier of a heart attack brought on by her anorexia. Willie still lived in the tiny house they had shared. The small amount of life insurance maintained the house and covered his basic living expenses. Even if he lost his job, he would have enough to exist on. But his earnings were earmarked for something else. Something invaluable. Something—given just a little more time—that might have provided Willie with a reason to live. Desserts.

Desserts were Willie's great passion. He gave up buying them after his mother died and he had to do his own grocery shopping. He couldn't stand the laughter chasing him down the aisles and into the checkout stand at the supermarket.

But no one laughed at sacks of special pastry flours, endless varieties of sugar, slabs of imported chocolate, quarts of whipping cream, the magical nuts and off-season fruits that can only be found in the expensive gourmet food stores. No one ridiculed the purchase of special cake pans and pastry marbles at exclusive uptown cookware shops. He wasn't a fat man in those places. He was a chef. A gourmet.

The transformation became complete in his home. He'd float through the narrow entry to his kitchen. The walls and cramped counterspace expanded and welcomed him. His clothing fit and his hair lay flat. He'd grow lighter, his senses more acute. Willie's pudgy fingers would dance nimbly as he measured out the ingredients for each confection. He never spilled or dropped anything. He felt as weightless as the meringues he whipped into tall peaks. He could hear the sound of a lemon souffle rising in the oven. The delectable aromas brought his taste buds to their knees as he sampled and adjusted each creation. Willie scorned written recipes, relying instead on his intuition and his palate for perfection.

No—no one laughed at the great chefs of the world. No matter what their size, they were artists. Willie had privately, anonymously, joined their ranks. He was as good as the best of them. And now, this one good thing in his life was being snatched away. Creating his masterpieces—once Willie's only possible escape—had ultimately been his downfall.

He sighed as he lumbered through the small living room that was filled with his mother's antiques. The spindly Philadelphia chairs, painted ebony with elaborate stencils of flowers and fruit, practically quivered as he passed by. The satin covered Duncan Phyfe sofa was certainly wide enough but way too shallow for his bulk. Willie had never been allowed to sit on these things as a child. The taboo had followed him into adulthood.

He checked the elaborate tea service set up on his portable table. The brilliant colors of the paper-thin Canton china glowed against the white linen cloth he had spread out. The Wallace silver gleamed in the light of the single candle he lit to brighten the afternoon gloom occasioned by the perpetually drawn curtains.

Willie admired his mother's elaborate cut-crystal cake plate on which he had arranged the two dozen almond cream tarts he had made that afternoon. There was enough cyanide in each one to drop a large man in his tracks. He'd hoarded quite a stockpile from his chemical factory job.

He rolled the table over in front of the bargain-basement loveseat that crouched against a wall away from the delicate antiques. It was the only chair in the house he could fit into. He decided to write the note while he waited for his tea water to heat.

The doorbell rang as he started across the room toward the writing desk. Willie ignored it and pulled a sheet of heavy, cream-colored paper from a polished shelf on the secretary. His mother had given him the stationary years ago. He never used it. He had no one to write to. His name, William Pardo, was embossed in heavy gold calligraphy at the top of the page. It would do nicely for his suicide note.

He headed back toward the kitchen ledge, the only surface he could lean on without breaking. The bell rang again. Someone pounded on the door.

"Hey, Willie!" a female voice screeched. "I know you're in there. Open up."

Dorel. Willie cringed, sighed heavily, and went to open the door. She'd lived next door to him for three years now and considered his kitchen a secondary grocery store. She wouldn't leave until she got what she wanted, but she wouldn't stay long either. Just once, he thought as he unbolted the door to let her in, just once he wished she would come to the door to share some trivial neighborhood gossip with him, offer him some coffee, or even ask him over to watch television. She was his only contact in the neighborhood and the closest thing he had to a friend. He yanked the door open.

Dorel Linden, formerly Dorothy Calvo, slouched in the doorway. She was thin as a boning knife with a nasty mouth to match. Her straight hair—dark brown and razored into someone's idea of retro-chic—angled around a face that was nothing but sharp corners and points. Facial potholes, left over from an adolescent sugar addiction, were paved over with a heavy pancake makeup that stopped abruptly at her chin.

"About time," she rasped as she sucked on a cigarette. "Got a girlfriend in here?" Smoke poured out of her as she laughed at her own wit.

Willie just stared at her. Waited for her demands.

It didn't take long. "I'm having some people over for a potluck tonight," she began.

Dorel continued talking, but Willie didn't hear a word she said. His heart almost stopped. His thoughts raced. She's inviting him to her party. He was ashamed for thinking ill of her, suspecting her motives. Briefly ashamed. The thrill of being invited washed all that out. A party. He could bring a fabulous dessert. It would be his last one before going on a diet. Everyone would crowd around him and smile. He'd make friends. He could tell them about his new diet and they'd all laugh sympathetically and exchange diet stories. Maybe they'd form a support group. They'd promise to phone each other in the dead of the night when the chocolate cake would begin its deadly siren's song. They'd encourage him, nurture him, while he battled for his health. He could even share his dream of becoming a great pastry chef. He didn't have to gorge anymore. He didn't have to kill himself. He had a reason to live. Someone cared. Dorel, his new best friend.

"Well?" she asked.

"I'd love to come, Dorel," he said. "I can whip up something really incredible for dessert. What time should I be there?"

Dorel skewered Willie with an annoyed look she quickly tried to mask.

"Weren't you listening to me? I came over to borrow some sugar for the coffee. No one else on the street is home." She smiled at him with poorly feigned regret. "I can't invite you, Willie. It's a party for my office staff."

She was lying, of course. Willie's curtains were always drawn, but he usually left the windows open for air. Two of his neighbors had stopped in front of his house earlier in the day while walking their dogs. He could hear every word they said as they encouraged their dogs to go on "Lardo Pardo's" lawn. They were discussing Dorel's neighborhood potluck that evening. Everyone had been invited. Everyone but Willie.

He just stared at Dorel's lying face. All the wonderful dreams of friendship, support, and a new life he'd owned for such a brief moment had vanished. His shoulders sagged back into his massive body. The Governor's call had come, but it was a wrong number.

"So how about it, Willie?" She didn't bother to disguise the irritation this time. "Can I have the sugar?"

Willie didn't answer her. He squeezed through his kitchen door, pulled the lid off the sugar canister and began scooping some sugar into a brown paper bag for her.

"Hey, these look great! What are they?"

Willie panicked. He twisted around and spilled some of the sugar on to the floor. He could see Dorel standing next to the loveseat.

"They're almond tarts, Dorel," he stammered. "I picked them up on my way home from work today."

Dorel's eyes shifted from the tarts—to Willie—to the tarts again.

"Gosh, Willie," she wheedled. "Would you let me have about twenty of them? We were all supposed to cook something, but I spent most of the night waiting for the police to kick out my no-good boyfriend. He busted up my bedroom and threatened me again. You just can't imagine what it's like to have someone you love turn on you."

Dorel lowered her head, passed a hand over her eyes and moved closer to the tarts. "It's too late to cancel my party, but I'm just too upset to make anything." She paused for a second and turned her face toward Willie. Her carefully arranged features formed a mask of dry-eyed tragedy. "You could help me, you know. I had an idea about these little tarts while we were talking. Wouldn't it be great if everyone thought I made them? Really make an impression on my boss. How about it?"

Willie was about to decline when he saw the look in her eye. He knew that look—coercion and disgust topped off with a heavy dose of contempt. He had seen it in his father's face before he left. It was the same one his mother had worn as she heaped gravied potatoes on his plate. He saw it when Dr. Barnes ordered him to undress for an exam. Roy hurled it at him every time Willie bumped into him behind the food counter at work. His neighbors—who didn't even know him—stared at his house that way. The whole world gave him that look. He shut his eyes for a moment to block her out.

"So?" The sharp inflection of her voice slashed through his reverie. "How about it?"

Willie opened his eyes and smiled, really smiled—for the first time in years.

"Sure, Dorel," he said as he glided easily through the doorway. His feet scraping through the sugar on the floor made a happy, scuffling noise like an old soft-shoe routine. "Take them all. They're small and I'm sure your friends will really like them. Here's a pastry box."

Willie reached into the hall closet and pulled out one of the pink cake boxes he'd been saving for ages. He handled the box with only the slightest pressure of his fingers on the edges. He'd hoped to fill it with his own creations one day and apply for a job in an exclusive restaurant as a pastry chef. This seemed like a much better use for it.

"That's okay," she said reaching for the tarts. "I'll just keep them on this fancy dish and return it tomorrow."

"Sorry, Dorel," he said as he intercepted her. Willie handed her the box and gently began to fill it. "Mother's things never leave the house." He threw the bag of sugar on to the top of the box. "Be sure to let me know how these work out."

"Sure, sure," she said as she ran out the door. She had already forgotten him.

Willie stared at the closed door for a second. Smiling, he turned around and sailed back into the kitchen.

"Revenge," he hummed to himself as he sifted out pastry flour. "Revenge," he sang out loud as he toasted the almonds for garnish. "Revenge," he laughed as he measured out the cyanide for the anonymous gifts to Roy and Dr. Barnes.

At last, Willie had a reason to live.

Revenge is sweet.

HOME COOKIN'

Lisa D. Williamson

The news of his death hit hard.

The fact that he had fallen down the cellar stairs and died in the fall wasn't so surprising: the house is old and the steps to the basement are steep and rickety.

"Oh God, Mom, how awful for you." I looked down from my six-foot-plus height at her, petite and still pretty despite the years with Dad.

"Well, it was quick," she answered bravely. "I tried to call, but you would insist on driving the whole way here. I didn't know how to get hold of you. But, we will go into all that and the . . . the arrangements later. I've decided we'll go on with Thanksgiving dinner. Your father would have liked that."

Dad had never liked anything she decided, but I didn't mention it. I somehow couldn't face the thought of a hearty dinner just yet, though. I told her I needed to sort things out, that I'd be back in an hour or so.

"I understand, dear," she said, standing on tiptoe to give me a kiss. "Just be back for dinner by 1:30."

I wandered through my hometown, recognizing old favorites: the sporting goods store, the drug store with the soda counter. On impulse, I ducked into an old favorite of my father's, the Village Tavern.

It was dark and murky. I found the bar, got a beer and groped my way to a booth. The place was pretty empty, this being Thanksgiving and all. An old man in the corner looked up, saw me, and heaved himself off his barstool.

"You won't remember me, but I'm Dr. Earp." He stuck out a gnarled hand. "Don't mind if I sit, do you?"

Since he was sitting by the end of his question, I made no objection. He had obviously started his holiday celebration a few hours earlier. His eyes were red and watery, his speech somewhat slurred.

"A danged shame about your father, boy. He was rough, but good as you can hope to find underneath."

I murmured something meaningless, hoping he'd go away and leave me to my thoughts. No such luck.

He was the one who had signed Dad's death certificate, and he felt compelled to discuss the whole thing with me. I fell into a rather comfortable haze, brought on by a second beer and the white noise of his conversation, so I only caught the tail end of it.

". . . the marks . . . the marks weren't right . . . something big and blunt, a good twenty–thirty pounds. But I told myself, Seth, I said, who could've done it? Only one there was Helen, and she's so tiny. Besides, she was upstairs getting your holiday dinner all organized. And with what? T'weren't nothing there. So I figured it had to be the stairs, or maybe the railing. Guess I did right, you think?"

"What? What did you say?" I must have scared him, because he blinked and, like an alarmed tortoise, withdrew from me. He shuffled back to his stool, muttering something about old fools and sleeping dogs.

Old fools is right, I thought, and I'd be a young fool if I paid any attention to this one. I looked at my watch, realized it was past one already, and headed back home.

As I walked in through the kitchen door, I could hear the pot lids rattling cheerfully against the steam and caught the myriad of odors that mean Thanksgiving to me: champ, medley, dressing, and bird. Or to the uninitiated: mashed potatoes with chives; parsnip, turnip, and carrot mash; stuffing; and turkey. I lifted some of the lids and sniffed appreciatively.

"Oh, just in time, dear."

I looked up to see Mom entering the kitchen, tightening her apron in back. She went to the fridge and took out some celery.

"Here, have a beer."

She handed me a can and a glass and went to the sink. She scrubbed the celery with her vegetable brush and began cutting thin strips. I smiled sadly, seeing a silly picture of the two of us, passing a condiment dish back and forth at dinner. I watched her deft hands as I poured my beer. She was short and slim, but years of country life had given her the forearms of a longshoreman. I listened absently to her cheerful chatter as I crossed the kitchen to the waste basket. Tossing in my empty can, I noticed the yellow plastic netting from the turkey, the kind with that convenient loop at the top for easy carrying.

"How big a bird did you get this year, Mom?" I asked, idly looking at the label. 27.3 pounds. It was going to be awfully strange, this first holiday without Dad. I guessed Mom would find it strange as well. Dad seemed to really come alive at holiday time; his snarling cruelties took on an even sharper edge when everything was festive.

"Oh, near enough to thirty pounds, I guess. I was just getting it out of the cellar freezer when your father . . ." Her face momentarily clouded. ". . . when your father came down."

"But I thought you were upstairs in the kitchen when it happened. That's what you told me."

"Did I, dear?" she asked vaguely. "Well, it's all done now."

She took the celery dish into the dining room and came back. Picking up two potholders, she opened the oven door. A burst of fragrant steam escaped.

A crazy thought came to me, so crazy a bubble of manic laughter escaped my lips. We're going to eat it, I thought. We're going to eat it and then no one will ever know.

She turned, holding the turkey out for my approval. It was nicely browned and still sizzling.

"Oh, isn't it beautiful, dear?" she exclaimed, her eyes gleaming. "Wouldn't your father just have *died* for a bird like this?"

A Way With Men

Mabel Maney

My aunt Maude says that if it rains this year like it did last summer, it's going to be the death of her. Maude says that rain is good for the crops, but her young elderberry trees will suffer if it storms. Last time it rained this much, whole trees were plucked right out of the earth and tossed down the road, leaving gaping shallow holes large enough for a person to lie in.

The common elderberry trees that ring our house never get very big. Their leaves are long but weak; their summer blooms white and small and delicate. When you crush the berries between your fingers, they leave your skin stained bright red. It won't come off for days, no matter how hard you scrub. Maude says it's a shame that something so pretty has such a fragile hold on the earth.

It's been raining on and off for a week. The sky is gray all day. Maude says it's just like the summer of the great Wisconsin rains of 1936 when she and her sister Mavis were ticket takers in a traveling circus; free meals and four dollars a week if attendance was good. A cyclone ripped the main tent right out of the ground and it flew away, never to be seen again.

When there's danger of a twister or a cyclone, go home and get into the basement. Don't leave the house, not even to go to the circus.

Maude says it gave her a funny feeling to see the old patched tent flying through the sky. It wasn't a real circus anyway, just some farm boys riding on old horses with ostrich feathers glued to their manes.

Maude has never been married. She says after being cooped up in a ticket booth for so many years, marriage is the last thing she can imagine. Mavis has been married three times. Each of her husbands suffered a sudden illness while on their honeymoon and was buried shortly thereafter. Mavis lives in Clear Lake now. My father says Mavis sure has a way with men. Then he always laughs.

Our neighbor Mrs. Thornburg says some women are just born to be unlucky in love. Mrs. Thornburg keeps yellow canaries in little cages on her windowsill. When she was newly married to Mr. Thornburg, she went to Hollywood on the train and got on the television show *Queen For A Day*. She won a washing machine, which still works nice, also a crown made of cardboard painted silver with glass bits glued on it. She keeps it on a special shelf above the washer. Once for my birthday she took it off the shelf and set it on my head. No one's allowed to touch it.

My father once sold televisions sets; then he sold shoes. The practical, old-lady kind that come in two colors—tan and gray. Tan for everyday and gray for dress-up, we supposed. It wasn't his best job, but it wasn't his worst. Lately he visits pretty regularly. He says he would like to take me on the road with him. He says I belong to him and not to Maude. He says the older I get the more I look like my mother, who's been gone longer than I remember.

Mrs. Thornburg, who's a good Catholic and not lapsed like us, says that when a person dies, their soul flies right out of their body. It's a scientific fact, she says. She read in the newspaper that nurses at a Catholic hospital in Chicago discovered their patients lost weight at the exact moment of death. Once a white flame was seen leaping from a dead man's chest and a nurse fainted.

Mrs. Thornburg says that souls are small and almost invisible, so you have to be quick if you want to see one. She says if your soul is pure, it will go right to heaven, and that's the best possible thing. Souls that have marks on them circle the earth, anxiously awaiting some kind of sign. Sometimes it comes too late, and they've already been pulled into hell.

When you hear a strange noise at night, what you think is the scraping of the box elder against the bedroom window, it could just as well be a fight over possession of someone's soul. Mrs. Thornburg says when we're asleep, the devil comes to earth to try and wrestle weak souls from the angels' grasp. Mrs. Thornburg says you have to keep one eye open for them, even when you're sleeping. Mrs. Thornburg knows all these things because her sister is a nun at a convent in Eau Claire.

Once when my father was selling ladies' toiletry items door-to-door he went to the convent in Eau Claire and knocked on the gate, but they wouldn't let him in. A salesman's smile is his ticket to heaven, he always says. Then he smiles.

The last time he was here he said not to listen to a thing Mrs. Thornburg says because she's crazy. And Maude's a sentimental old fool. He says he would like to take me on the road with him. He says I belong to him and not to Maude. He says the older I get the more I look like my mother.

Everyone always asks Maude why doesn't she plant something sturdier, knowing how it rains around here. Every year we drive down the street picking up battered elderberry trees. Sometimes they can't be saved, and soon as it's dry enough we build a fire out back for them. Maude cries when the flames get high and the branches blacken, then crumble into ash.

My grandfather was a farmer. When one of his dogs became crippled from age he would take it to the woods and shoot it. We have three dogs: an apricot poodle named Goldie, a little sheep dog named Lily, and Stella, a scruffy tan dog Maude says is probably part terrier. Lily is old now and I have to carry her upstairs with me at night. Maude says when it's her time we'll bury her in a box under the oak out back.

When my father comes here, Maude makes a bed for him on the old red davenport on the back porch. Lately he visits pretty regularly. He says it's not safe for me and Maude to live here all alone. He says it's about time we had a man around the house. He waits until Maude is asleep and comes to my room in the attic. He always tells me the same story.

My grandfather would take his gun and the old dog would follow him into the woods, happy that of all the dogs, he had been chosen for the rare treat of being alone with the master.

My father says Lily reminds him of my grandfather's favorite sheep dog, Ruby. After my grandfather shot Ruby, she got up and tried to follow him home, so he had to break her neck. My father says dogs are dogs. He says when a dog is old there's nothing you can do but take it out to the woods. My father says Maude lets me live in a dream world. He says Maude had better wake up.

My father says he would like to take me on the road with him. He says I belong to him and not to Maude. He says the older I get, the more I look like my mother.

At night when he comes to visit he always tells me the same story. The old dog would follow my grandfather out to the woods. My father says he doesn't mean to hurt me, but he always does. Later he always says he's sorry.

I asked Mrs. Thornburg if dogs have souls. She says she'll ask her sister next time she sees her. Visiting hours are strict at the convent, and sometimes Mrs. Thornburg doesn't see her sister for months. Maude went to school with a girl who took a vow of silence. She hasn't spoken in over twenty years, not even to her family.

My father has a new job in Menasha, so he can see me more. "Just you wait," he told Maude last time.

The other day I found Maude crying downstairs where she does the wash. I think Maude's sad to see the elderberry trees struggling so. It's good that Mavis has come to visit. Maude hasn't been sleeping well and she can use the company.

Maude says I'm to sleep with her tonight. Mavis is staying in my room so she can hear the rain on the roof. It will be a surprise to my father, who doesn't like Mavis. Mavis says it will probably stop raining tomorrow, so tonight is the best night for it.

My father always says Mavis has a way with men. Then he laughs. The sky has been dark all day. My father is due here late tonight, but we'll already be in bed. I'm sleeping with Maude tonight so Mavis can stay in my room. My father will be awfully surprised.

On Fridays Mrs. Thornburg shows filmstrips in her living room, folding her laundry while we watch various religious themes projected onto her white nubby-cotton draperies, the ones she made herself with a little bit of help from Mavis last time she was here. Mrs. Thornburg says Mavis has a real talent for working with her hands, but it's too bad she can't keep a husband.

This week's film shows Saint Florian being swept away by a raging river, but he keeps on preaching. He is the patron saint of floods. It's starting to rain again, so we drop to our knees and offer him our devotion. Mrs. Thornburg says that sometimes you must suffer in order to placate God for the wrongs done by others.

Today Mavis and Maude dug a big ditch in the back yard. It's long and narrow and deep. It keeps filling with water, but Maude says it will be dry enough for what she has in mind. Maude says this time she's going to plant something so deep it's going to stay put.

My father is due by tonight. He's working nearby so he can see me more. He says the older I get, the more I look like my mother. He says I belong to him and not to Maude.

Maude says it's time for us to go to bed. Mavis is going to sleep in my room so she can hear the rain on the roof. I hope my father doesn't scare Mavis when he finds her in my bed, instead. My father always says Mavis has a way with men. Then he always laughs.

Maude says this time she's going to plant something so deep, even the heaviest rain won't take it from the ground. Mrs. Thornburg will be happy to know that Maude has finally come to her senses. Mrs. Thornburg says Maude has a good heart, but she's not so sure about the condition of her soul.

American Gothic

Linda K. Wright

She sat, rocking in her chair, clacking her knitting needles. He was sitting in his easy chair, smoking his pipe and reading the newspaper article aloud to her. She would occasionally stop the flow of his words and ask him to read a line again. When he finished the article, he put the newspaper down, relit his pipe, and said, "Guess he'll be coming to see us now."

"Yes," she sighed, "this would be the first place he'd stop. Better not lock the door tonight, he'll just smash one of the windows. Best he come in without messing the place up."

She paused to concentrate on picking up a dropped stitch. He had read the story to her quite thoroughly, but she asked again, nevertheless, "How long ago did he break out?"

"Paper says sometime early this morning. He killed two of the attendants who were escorting him back to his room after he visited the doctor."

She glanced at the clock on the mantelpiece. It was a little after seven.

"If he took the first train out he'd have arrived at the station an hour ago. Guess he's out there now." She nodded her head in the direction of the window facing the yard.

"No use in trying to phone the Sheriff—lines are cut by now."

They heard a twig snap, and the sound of footsteps in the leaf-cluttered yard.

"That's him."

"Yep, that's him," he said, putting his pipe back in his mouth, picking up the newspaper, and settling down in his easy chair.

The front door opened and the draft blew the ball of yarn across the floor.

Jessie

Katherine V. Forrest

I

"It's a bad time for you to visit, Kate," Sheriff Jessie Graham offered in quiet apology.

"I'm glad to be here, Jess," Kate replied with equal quietness. "I know how close you are to Walt. Right now you need your friends."

Kate Delafield, sipping coffee from a styrofoam cup, sat beside Jessie Graham's desk in one of the plain wooden chairs the county of Alta Vista provided for visitors to its sheriff's station at Seacliff. She said to Jessie, "As I recall, he helped you get this job."

Jessie nodded. "I owe it to him."

"You say he disappeared Friday. Any theories about why—or where he might be?"

Jessie contemplated Kate Delafield, the strong face framed by fine graying hair, the intelligent, somber light blue eyes. Kate had last stopped here for a visit more than two years ago, and Anne had been with her. Anne's accident, her death, had happened two months after that, and Jessie had not learned of it until a week after the funeral. . . .

"Woman, you're on vacation," Jessie growled, reaching to place a hand over Kate's arm, and pointedly surveying Kate's jeans and the hooded white sweatshirt adorned with a small LAPD insignia. "You're not four hours out of that smog-ridden cesspool, I'm not about to—"

"The smog's a little better in L.A. these days, Jess," Kate said with a faint smile. She slouched back into the wooden chair as if it were comfortably cushioned, and crossed an ankle over a knee. She picked up her cup of coffee. "My friend, tell me about it."

"It's a hell of a thing." For the first time in two days Jessie felt the pressure within her ease, felt a sense of comfort. She pushed herself back from her desk, rested a foot on an open desk drawer, folded her arms across her brown uniform shirt. She said in a rush of words, "There's no damn sense to it, Kate. I played cards with the man and four friends of ours Friday night. I swear he was the same as always. He left my place making jokes and waving twenty-seven dollars in winnings; he'd taken most of those dollars from me. The next morning Walt's wife calls me, claims that in the middle of that very same night he'd taken off in pouring down rain with a bag of money under his arm, without his car, and nobody's seen hide nor hair of him since. There's no *sense* to it."

Kate shook her head sympathetically; her eyes narrowed in scrutiny of her friend. "Any theories, Jess?"

"Theoretically," Jessie said with all the confidence she could muster, "he's a missing person. He may just turn up like a lot of them do." Then she felt a stinging behind her eyes and looked quickly away. "Kate—dammit, Kate, I know in my gut he's dead."

When she could control her voice she said almost angrily, "My gut feelings don't always turn out to be fact." She forced a semblance of a grin. "I had a gut feeling about Irene, too. That we'd be together forever."

"I know the feeling." Kate gestured at the case file on Jessie's desk. "Could I take a look?" Jessie handed it over. "Tell me everything, Jess. Everything you've got, right down to the fine hairs."

Jessie nodded gratefully. Then scowled, remembering the Saturday morning two days before in Walt Kennon's house.

♦

Velma Kennon had been seated in an armchair in the immaculate living room, her red-checked apron clashing violently with the pale lavender of the upholstery. She pulled a gray cardigan loosely around her shoulders and said in soft, reluctant tones, "He had me draw out the ten thousand from our savings Friday."

Jessie's voice was sharp with skepticism. "Why'd he have you do that? Why wouldn't he do it himself?"

"Maybe it was his way of telling me." Her voice broke. "I think he was in some kind of trouble."

If she expects me to fall for this horse manure . . .

"I *know* him," Jessie said. "You're Walt's wife—but it's only been a year for you, Velma." There was hostility in her tone that she had not intended, and she added more gently, "I grew up knowing the man; we've been close friends ever since I came back to Seacliff. I *know* Walt. There's no sense to this."

Velma picked up a corner of her checked apron and dabbed at a cheek. "Well, I thought Walter loved me."

Jessie asked with renewed brusqueness, "What'd Walt say he needed the ten thousand for?"

"He said I should just trust him." The voice throbbed with injury. "Said he'd explain it all later. I think he needed that money to pay someone off. I think he was in some kind of serious trouble. Maybe trouble from back when he was sheriff here. And whoever it was took him somewhere and . . . maybe the ocean."

Jessie pushed herself to her feet, shifted her hands down to rest them just above the wide belt and holster. "He'll have to be missing forty-eight hours before it's official. But I'd like to have a look around now if it's all right with you, Velma."

Velma uncrossed her thin ankles and rose to her full height, not much over five feet. Her dark eyes were reproachful. "I'd never have called you if I didn't want you looking into this any way you can. Go right ahead, look everywhere."

Jessie radioed for a car to pick up Cowan, the deputy who had accompanied her; she wanted to be alone as she sifted through the possessions of Walter Kennon. She knew she might spot something odd, some little thing Cowan could miss.

After Cowan was gone, she sat in her sheriff's car trying to collect her thoughts and fight down an almost paralyzing foreboding. Not for a moment did she believe one detail of Velma Kennon's story.

In two days of hearings before the seven commissioners of Alta Vista County, Jessie had learned all she needed to know about the character of Walt Kennon. Ten years a retired sheriff, he had challenged the commissioners to ignore Jessie's superior record, her solid years of experience in police work in both Los Angeles and Alta Vista County, her administrative ability, her leadership qualities. Jessie knew that she owed the position she had held for the past year and a half entirely to Walt Kennon.

Groping for objectivity, she reviewed the facts she readily knew about him. He was sixty-four. He'd been released from Veterans' Hospital in '46, some months after the war. Had finished his education at Cal Poly in San Luis Obispo, then come back to Seacliff and taken up police work, rising to the position of sheriff. But the shrapnel fragments still scattered throughout both his legs and the persistent severe pain had led to his early retirement twelve years later. Of his wartime experiences she remembered him saying only, "Duty. Loyalty. A man owes it."

He had settled into the town of his birth just as Jessie had—like a thirsty plant sinking deep roots. And like Jessie, had grumbled at every evidence of the oceanside town's growth. Walt's only vacations had been to Los Angeles to visit a brother afflicted with emphysema, and he returned each time even more contemptuous of big city life. He was Jessie's kind of person: quiet and leather-tough, his friendship a hard-won prize, a man who kept to himself until some interior principle signaled him to speak—as he had for Jessie, as he had again just recently when a consortium of builders tried to force re-zoning of a section of mobile homes occupied by elderly residents.

Her mind dark with apprehension, Jessie climbed out of her car and went back into Walt Kennon's house. In the bedroom she inspected Walt's familiar plaid shirts and windbreakers, the baggy corduroys he usually wore around town and to her card games, his khaki gardening pants, the fleece-lined jacket for the few really chill days of winter, the well-worn cardigan sweaters, the one good blue suit with the white shirt protected by plastic. Like herself, Walt had few clothes; he preferred what was tried and true and comfortable. Jessie noted that the clothes Walt had worn the night before night—gray corduroys, a blue plaid Pendleton shirt, a black plastic raincoat—were not in the closet. Everything there seemed orderly, undisturbed.

As did Velma's closet. The contents were modest: housedresses and cotton robes, a few skirts and frilly blouses, three good woolen dresses. But inside several large, zippered plastic bags were smartly styled suits and dinner dresses, high-heeled sandals, and evening shoes stored in plastic compartments—all of these apparently relics from Velma's past, and all of them useless in quiet, informal Seacliff.

Jessie was glad to move her scrutiny from the bedroom to an area less evocative of Velma and Walt Kennon's marriage. In the living room, dozens of *Field and Stream* back issues on the inconspicuous bottom shelf of the small bookcase were the only concrete traces of Walt Kennon. In heterosexual marriage, Jessie mused as she browsed around the carefully appointed room, precious little of a house ever really belonged to the male; his part of the closets maybe, and the yard and garage. The living room *always* belonged to the woman. Yet there was no evidence of Velma in this room, Jessie realized—or anywhere else. Odd that the house had changed so little during the entire year of Walt Kennon's second marriage.

Remembering how swiftly she'd made her own quarters austere again after the three-year disaster with Irene in Los Angeles, Jessie moved into the den adjoining the living room. She looked at a framed photo of Velma and Walt on the small, leather-topped desk, and admitted that she disliked Velma Kennon intensely.

She'd accepted her at first, and willingly. Walt had been five years alone with his grief, and it was good to see him happy. And Velma was a pretty woman, and vivacious. But the buoyancy had soon left Walt's step. And Velma's prettiness and high energy seemed to fade with each succeeding month of her marriage to Walt. Only once in the past year had Walt invited the Friday night poker group to his house—when Velma was away visiting her parents in Garden Grove. Walt and Velma seemed to be two people who had leeched the vitality from each other.

Jessie could easily account for Walt's faithfulness to this joyless marriage—the same reason he had never questioned his wartime obligation: *Duty. Loyalty. A man owes it.* As for Velma's reason, it appeared to be the classic one: she had no means of support other than Walt Kennon.

Jessie opened to top drawer of the desk. She found a twenty-five thousand dollar insurance policy, Velma Kennon beneficiary; a copy of the deed to property in Santa Barbara which had been signed over to Bergan Construction Company on January ninth—only two months ago; and a bank book. She opened the bank book. It showed a ten thousand dollar withdrawal made this past Friday and a current balance of two hundred and eighty-six thousand dollars; two hundred and fifty thousand of that amount had been deposited on January nineteenth.

Jessie gaped at the number for only an instant. She knew all the surface details of Walt's life; he'd willingly shared them, but never had she heard him speak specifically of his finances. No more than he had ever shared his grief and loneliness for Alice, or talked of how his legs had been shot from under him during the assault on Guadalcanal. He'd muttered about the cost of living—had grumbled at the card game about expensive repairs to his Toyota—but she knew he contributed to the support of his chronically ill brother, and he always seemed to have sufficient money. She had assumed that he lived in relative comfort on a combination of military and police pensions and social security.

"Velma," Jessie called, "could you please come in here a minute?"

Velma glanced blandly at the bank book. "It's Walter's money. His savings, and proceeds from selling a house in Santa Barbara that belonged to his first wife." Her voice took on bitterness. "When my first husband died, I didn't have two thin dimes left after probate."

Jessie tapped the bank book with a fingernail. "Says here it's your money as well, Velma. As joint tenant." Then she added reflectively, "I remember about that Santa Barbara house—Alice wouldn't sell it. Amazing it was worth so much money."

"The land it's on was re-zoned commercial years ago. She never did one thing with that place for years," Velma said harshly. "Never even raised the rent of the people living there. Him either, after she died."

"Alice liked the tenants," Jessie said mildly, picking up the executed deed, turning it over in her hands, her mind lighted with the image of Alice Kennon. Genial, comfortable Alice, with mink brown hair that had suddenly gone gray and then whitened over the years, and hazel eyes always radiating humor and spirit, conveying that everything about Jessie—everything—was just fine with her. She had given Walt Kennon a glow of quiet contentment for twenty-six years, until the diagnosis of pancreatic cancer. Just a scant six weeks after that, Jessie Graham had borne one of the heaviest burdens of her life—the casket of Alice Kennon to her gravesite in Rolling Hills Cemetery.

Replacing the documents, Jessie brushed a finger along the lock mechanism on the drawer. She bent down to examine it. "Walt mentioned a couple of weeks ago he'd made out a will, to make sure his brother was taken care of. One of those handwritten wills. Holographic, they call them."

Velma looked startled. "I don't know about any will." She added with belligerence, "I never saw it."

"Drawer's been forced open," Jessie stated, watching her. "You know why that'd be?"

Two thin furrows formed between the penciled brows. "The drawer's never once been locked so far as I know. I don't know what anybody'd take."

Maybe that will.

The yard was neat, well tended, the grass wet and spongy under Jessie's feet. The pain in Walt's legs had limited how much he could do, but he loved gardening, and well-cultivated flower beds bordered the front of the house and the side hedge. Last night's heavy rain had separated and caked the dirt around the bushes.

Jessie walked up the driveway past the house and opened the garage. The gray Toyota was parked against one wall; garden utensils lined the opposite wall. A few woodworking

tools lay on a scarred bench. She picked up a plastic hood
and covered the circular saw that Walt used to cut his
firewood. A movement caught her eyes; she glanced over to
catch the flutter of curtain at the kitchen window.

So Velma was watching her. With heightened senses she
examined the garage minutely, donning a pair of Walt's work
gloves to pick up and study each tool. She found nothing
unusual until she came to a well-used but very clean shovel.
At the kitchen window, Velma Kennon watched openly as
Jessie studied it. She replaced the shovel and went into the
house.

Velma stood at the kitchen counter slicing a tomato; its
rich, earthy odor reached Jessie. It occurred to her that she
had always seen Velma Kennon in a colorless dress covered
by a red-checked apron with big pockets.

Jessie said evenly, "That's a mighty clean shovel out there
in the garage."

"Walter left it out in the rain last week," Velma said, her
eyes on the knife slicing through the ripe red tomato.

"Didn't rain last week," Jessie informed her.

"Well, whenever it last did," Velma said in exasperation.

Jessie said, not bothering to soften her skepticism,
"Being careless with one of his tools isn't something Walt
would do."

Velma's knife stilled. She stared at Jessie, then said with
asperity, "It doesn't sound like Walter to just go off and
disappear without a trace, either."

"Don't think that's what he did."

She locked eyes with Velma Kennon. Velma's unreadable
dark stare did not waver. Finally Jessie said, "Could I trouble
you for the keys to the Toyota?"

She followed Velma into the living room. Velma picked
up her purse from the desk.

"Could I trouble you to look at the purse," Jessie said.
"Just routine."

"Of course," Velma said with distinct sarcasm, and
thrust the leather bag at Jessie, her fingers rigid. "As I recall,
I think I've got thirty-two dollars in bills, and a little change."

Jessie did not reply. Of course Velma wouldn't be stupid
enough to carry any of that ten thousand dollars in her
purse. Removing one object at a time, she carefully placed

on the desk a comb, wallet, lipstick, compact, metal nail file, package of tissues, ballpoint pen, checkbook. The checkbook register showed ordinary transactions.

"The ten thousand," Jessie said, "What denominations did the bank give you?" She examined the zippered pocket and lining of the black leather purse.

"Five hundred in twenties," Velma muttered, her lips in a thin tight line, "the rest in fifties and hundreds."

Jessie nodded. "That's quite a wad of cash." She handed the purse back to Velma. "I'll let you put everything back the way you want. We have to look at everything, Velma. Just routine," she added absently, thinking that Walt had bought chips at the poker game with two tens.

Jessie unlocked the car. The Toyota Celica showed the usual signs of five-year wear and smelled of Walt's pipe tobacco. She added the powerful beam of her flashlight to the morning sunlight and examined the interior. She'd impound the car; Elbert and Ron over at Martinsville would go over it thoroughly. But there were no visible stains. Of any kind.

Deep in thought, she walked slowly to her own car and replaced the flashlight in its sprocket. Money and property were the reasons for many marriages—and the motive for the vast majority of crime. Most people would say Velma was not the type to kill, but Jessie knew anybody was the type. Knew it from those years of police work down in Los Angeles and fifty-two years of plain, hard living. Only their Maker knew why people did the things they did.

Something had happened to Walt—and whatever it was, Velma had done it. Of that Jessie was certain. She shifted her gunbelt, adjusting the heavy holster, wishing she could do the same for her leaden heart. Velma had done something to him and taken him somewhere to dispose of him.

But where? And how? It just wasn't physically possible for a hundred and ten pound woman of nearly fifty to do much with a man Walt's size, certainly not against his will, and not if he was dead weight, either. Walt had become heavier recently; he was a good hundred and seventy pounds, maybe more. He'd joked ruefully about it just last night as he helped himself to potato chips and dip at the poker game. . . .

Another memory of the poker game leaped into Jessie's mind. She whirled and trotted back to the Toyota. Walt's complaint about expensive repairs to the Toyota—he'd picked up the car on the way to the poker game; he'd had it in for a brake relining and carburetor work, plus routine maintenance. . . .

Jessie yanked open the car door, knelt to scan the Union Oil sticker on the door frame, then compared the mileage figure written there by the service station to the mileage on the speedometer, jotting the numbers in her note pad. Velma Kennon watched from the kitchen window.

From the time Walt had picked up the car, it had been driven two miles and whatever number of tenths that were unaccounted for. Gil's Union Oil Station was around the corner from the Kennon house; Walt had driven from there to Jessie's house for poker. Based on the time Velma had given as Walt's arrival home, he'd come directly here from the poker game. By marking off those distances in her own car she could tell if Walt's car had been driven after he'd arrived at his house. One thing she knew for sure: if this car *had* been driven, it hadn't been driven far.

Concealing her excitement, Jessie clumped back into the house. "Velma," she asked, "you drive that car after Walt got home last night?"

"Why . . . no. Of course not."

"I'm sealing it off, impounding it for the time being. I'll say goodbye to you for now."

Velma wiped her hands on her checked apron. "Something bad's happened to him," she said. "I know it."

I'll bet you do.

"I guarantee," Jessie said, her tone heavy and ominous, "I'll find out. One way or the other, I'll find out."

She had turned then and stalked out to her police car.

II

Jessie had taken Kate to an early dinner at the Sandpiper, a weathered clapboard restaurant on a steep hillside overlooking Seacliff and the Pacific. She restrained herself from supplying more details of Walt Kennon's disappearance while Kate gazed at a bank of fog drifting its way in over the horizon, over white-capped swells of gray-blue ocean.

"As good a career as you had in L.A.," Kate said musingly, "I can see what compelled you to come back here."

Jessie smiled, and realized that she had not smiled in the past three days. "Much as I don't understand it, Kate, I see that you belong where you are, too. They need the best cops they can find down there in that nether side of hell."

Smiling, Kate picked up her scotch. "You don't get lonely up here, Jess, away from any sort of . . . activity?"

"Gay women, you mean." Jessie refrained from pointing out that Kate herself was on vacation alone. "We do have gay people here—hell, we're everywhere. Seacliff has fourteen thousand population now; it's a fair-sized place. A few folks know about me. . . . Some of them have long memories. I was chasing after girls in this town from the time I was six."

She chuckled along with Kate. "I'm private about myself just naturally. But I can't say I'm all that careful, even though some people here would jump at any reason to see me gone. They can't abide the idea of a woman sheriff, let alone—"

Jessie broke off to Kate's raised hand. Their first course, clam chowder, had arrived. Intoxicated by the aroma, Jessie dipped her spoon eagerly into the rich meaty creaminess, realizing that she had scarcely eaten since Saturday. As the waitress moved away, Jessie continued, wolfing down the chowder as she spoke, "I'll tell you the truth. My time with Irene told me one thing plain as day—I'm cut out to be a bachelor. I'm still your perfectly normal queer," she added with an embarrassed grin, "I do love women. I drive up to San Francisco now and again and get in some girl chasing. But this town is my family, I've got roots here, and responsibility, good friends—" She broke off and put down her soup spoon. Walt's disappearance was again like an iron weight in her stomach, displacing further desire for food.

"Tell me about the Kennon car." Kate's voice was dry, businesslike. "I assume it checked out clean?"

Jessie's smile was inward. Kate had not changed much; when her mind was locked into the details of a case, she spared limited attention for even such distractions as spectacular views of the Pacific or general conversation.

"No traces of blood," Jessie answered, "not in the car or on any of the tools. And Velma was made joint tenant on the savings account the week after Walt married her. Walt's the kind to do something like that."

Kate finished the last spoonful of her chowder, pushed the bowl away. She steepled her fingers and contemplated Jessie over them. "That's a point, Jess. If you're right about your gut feeling, then the motive here figures to be money, pure and simple. Since she's joint tenant, why would she do anything to Walt? Why wouldn't she just clean out that account and take off?"

Jessie nodded. "It's a good point. But I've figured out a couple of reasons. Velma doesn't seem the type to run even if she knew how to cover her tracks, and that's a lot harder to do in these days of computers. She'd have to cover her tracks awfully well with Walt after her, him being an ex-cop. I think she'd figure he'd track her down. She wouldn't feel safe for a minute."

"And if she simply divorced him," Kate mused, "she probably wouldn't come out with much of a settlement, considering the length of their marriage."

Jessie moved her soup bowl aside and pulled a folded sheet from the Kennon case file, a real estate map of Seacliff. "I've measured mileage to the exact tenth, Kate. Drove from Gil's Union Station to my house, then back to Walt's. I've got to think he came as direct as he could to my place—Gil at the station said Walt picked the car up at six-fifty-five, five minutes before the station closed. Walt arrived just after seven, like he usually did, and I've got four other witnesses to prove it."

"And afterward," Kate contributed, "aside from Velma's statement about when he arrived home, he wouldn't have reason to go anywhere. It was pouring rain—"

"And everything in town was closed, anyway," Jessie concluded. "So I got one and eight-tenths miles clicked off what Walt drove. That leaves an extra two tenths to account for, plus whatever other tenths were on there because the gas station only wrote down the whole number. Meaning Walt or Velma drove the car half of that distance, and Velma drove it back the other half."

Jessie extracted a pen from her uniform shirt pocket with the east of habit. "Here's the Kennon house." She indicated a point on the map in the center of a circle inscribed in pencil. "I took a compass and measured and drew this circle around the Kennon house—"

Kate reached for the map, studied it closely. Jessie said, "Most of it's residential."

"True," Kate said, "but there's some vacant land in here, Jess, and part of a cemetery."

"Rolling Hills Cemetery," Jessie said with a nod. "Alice Kennon's buried just on the other side of my circle. The cemetery's all grass, kept perfect, just like a lawn, I checked it out Sunday. And all that vacant land, I walked every bit of it, Kate. I looked at every damn square inch."

"You said it rained hard Friday night," Kate pointed out. "Heavy rain could cover up traces of a grave."

Jessie looked at her soberly. "I'll tell you the truth. I don't expect to find a grave. I mean, how could a little thing like Velma Kennon dig a grave? Anybody who's ever put a shovel into the ground can tell you uncultivated earth is like digging into cement. Earth wet from rain is like lifting a pile of rocks."

Their food arrived. Jessie looked at her swordfish with indifference. Kate sprinkled lemon on her lobster, then cut off a piece and munched on it as she continued her study of the real estate map.

Jessie said, "Let me fill you in about the other leads I checked out."

◆

"Sheriff Graham," the young teller had said nervously, "I gave Mrs. Kennon just what she asked for—"

"I know you did, Sarah. Now just relax," Jessie said in her most reassuring tones. "There's no problem about it at all. Were any of the bills in series?"

Sarah nodded. "But that much money in cash, I had to take it from the PG&E payroll, and that's close onto a hundred fifty thousand dollars, so there's no telling which of those bills I gave her."

Disappointed, Jessie said, "Thank you, Sarah. You call me now if you see any transaction Mrs. Kennon makes that's unusual, all right? Confidential, you have my word."

Jessie interviewed Ms. Neville, the librarian, who had telephoned Saturday afternoon as word of Walter Kennon's disappearance spread around town.

"It was six weeks ago, Sheriff." Ms. Neville peered at Jessie over the narrow rectangles of her reading glasses. "She never did check anything out. Every day for a week she came in here. And hasn't been back since." Her words were a sibilant, penetrating whisper in the single-room cavern that was Seacliff's public library, crowded and murmurous at this mid-afternoon hour on the weekend. "Can't say what she was reading, either. And that's what seemed so suspicious. She'd just put her book right back up on the shelf and move off if I came anywhere near."

The librarian's reproachful frown deepened. "Why would anybody care if another person saw what she was reading?"

Maybe she just flat resented your nosiness, Jessie thought. But she said gently, "Ms. Neville, can you tell me what general section she spent her time in?"

"The sciences. Anatomy. Medicine."

♦

Jessie cut several pieces from her swordfish, moved them around on her plate. "I'll tell you what else I did. I talked to everybody in the Kennon neighborhood—nothing. I ran a check on Velma Kennon's background—nothing. I sent urgent inquiries to every doctor and pharmacy in Alta Vista county. All I've turned up so far is a Darvon prescription when Walt had dental surgery."

Jessie took a forkful of baked potato. "I'll tell you, Kate, I'm baffled. I can't figure what Velma did or how she did it. Right now my theory . . ." She thrust the forkful of potato down in recoil from the images. "I think maybe she's chopped him up and got a piece tucked here and there." She braced, expecting incredulous laughter.

But Kate said firmly, "Jess, put that nightmare out of your head. I'm not claiming this woman doesn't have the alligator mentality it takes to do such a thing; we both know better. But look at your own body, think about all those quarts of blood. Imagine anybody trying to cut through bone and muscle. Imagine the kidneys, the intestines. With all respect, Jess—"

Jessie nodded hurriedly, feeling both foolish and immensely relieved. "Got to be an answer to this, Kate. Got to be."

Kate said, "Why don't I take a few bites of that swordfish you don't want?"

Jessie cut a large section from her fish. "The rest of this'll be a nice treat for Damon, my cat."

Kate nodded absently, her eyes once more on the Pacific. "Before we go to your place, I'd like you to drive me around the circle on this map. While it's still light."

III

Velma Kennon sat in her living room sipping tea, the day's *Courier* in her lap. But she was watching the patrol car, a black menace drifting along her street. Having passed the house twice, it would circle the block and come back once more. And a half hour from now repeat the process. Velma knew the habits of Seacliff's Sheriff's Department well; she had been under its close surveillance for three days.

With an irritated shrug she unfolded the *Courier*. Her eyes were instantly drawn by a name in a small headline down the page:

Former D.A.R. Chapter Pres.
Margaret Paxton Dies Here

She shook the paper open and scanned the short article extolling the accomplishments of Margaret Paxton, wife of the recently deceased Grant Paxton, then turned to the obituary page. The notice was almost identical to the one six days ago that had branded itself into her memory. Chilled, she dropped the paper back into her lap, stared out at the black police car cruising back past the house.

Not much longer, she reassured herself, sipping the hot, bracing tea. It would be only a matter of days before Sheriff Jessie Graham could no longer justify detaining her in Seacliff, before the sheriff would have to pursue her all the way to the coast of Florida if she wanted to continue her useless surveillance. A few years from now Velma Gardiner

Kennon would be the stuff of memory and legend in this town, the suspected murderess who had somehow conjured away the body of her husband.

Soon . . . it would all happen soon, and exactly as she'd planned. She had a nice solid nest egg now, and the day would come when she'd have even more—when Walter was declared dead and his life insurance paid off, and the title to the house would clear as well. A few more days and she'd have her freedom. After two years of pure misery, she'd earned it.

Never again would she suffer the humiliation of facing the future without resources. She would be able to forget those months of paralysis after Johnny's heart attack and the stunning news of his insolvency, when all the security she'd taken for granted for nearly thirty years had been wiped out. And the bitter months afterward when she'd been forced to live on the proceeds from her few good pieces of jewelry, when she'd learned how friendships just melted away once you were in trouble. And the job she'd been forced to accept as cashier in the dining room of The Duquesne, a hotel frequented by traveling salesmen and the women who found its dining room and bar convenient for assignations with those salesmen.

Walter Kennon had been an anomaly in such surroundings, pure chance bringing him there for the ten days of his visit with his ill brother. His interest in her had been tentative, shy and awkward; and she, having by this time taken cold-eyed stock of her situation, knew that marrying a man like the colorless, uninteresting Walter Kennon was probably about as well as she could do.

When he said she resembled his deeply mourned Alice, she had laid siege to Walter Kennon's affections by asking myriad questions about Alice, then pretending to be like her in every way she could devise. To her despair, Walter had returned to Seacliff after those ten days—but a month later reappeared to sheepishly propose marriage. That very same day she had resigned her detested job and, in triumph, traveled back with him to Seacliff.

But the town was slow-paced and quiet beyond all imagining. The spring and summer months of cloudy, foggy weather were depressing, unmitigated by the presence of the ocean; and the modest stucco or frame houses and their ordinary inhabitants were equally depressing. Her first husband had loved to socialize, to dance and drink; Walter Kennon sternly disapproved of alcohol, and looked forward only to his weekly poker game. Of all her pretense before their marriage, he was most unforgiving of the lie that she, like Alice, knew the game of poker and loved to play it.

But, deadly dull as Walter Kennon might be, he was, she conceded, kind and decent, and a good provider. She lived comfortably, if not agreeably.

In the first days of their marriage, he had shown her the contents of the locked desk drawer. "So you can rest easy about everything," he told her. "There'll be plenty enough for you, but I've written out this will making it a condition my brother Ralph's taken care of, too. I've made Jessie Graham executor. I'm depending on you both."

She had agreed, of course. She seldom disagreed, argued even more rarely. As the waif taken under this wing, any wishes of hers were subordinate to his decisions, and in his house she could not so much as move a pillow from sofa to chair without him moving it back. The ghost of Alice Kennon pervaded every room including the bedroom: Walter was indifferent to her physically.

Every aspect of their marriage was a sham; and her status in the life of this man, her distinct inferior, added a fresh layer of gall to all her other humiliations. Walter Kennon had married her only to keep his memories alive, to serve as a reflection of his enshrined Alice.

Smothered by her life, without any acceptable alternative, she daydreamed of moving back to Los Angeles to flaunt economic independence under the noses of the "friends" who had deserted her; she yearned to live independently amid the bright lights and energy of a major city. She longed for freedom unencumbered by Walter Kennon.

Then the letter from Bergan Construction Company had arrived. The company was interested in the property in Santa Barbara, prepared to make an offer. There was a toll-free eight-hundred number to call.

Walter had crumpled the letter, thrown it into the trash. "Alice's parents left her that house. The Herreras, they've lived there for years. Alice promised they could stay so long as they pay the taxes and upkeep on the place. I'm bound to keep that promise."

She had fished out the letter and called the toll-free number the following day. And learned that the land was now re-zoned, and Bergan Construction would offer a quarter of a million dollars clear cash, the buyer paying all expenses of the sale. Stunned by the magnitude of the offer, she explained the situation. Perhaps, Jack Bergan suggested, with Mrs. Kennon's approval, and provided he had her cooperation in the matter of selling the property to him, he himself might talk to the tenants. Perhaps they could be persuaded to move out on their own. . . .

Two weeks later a terse communication had arrived from Mr. and Mrs. Raul Herrera. At the end of the month they would be vacating the home they had lived in for nearly thirty years. The brevity of the note, its coldness, had bewildered, then hurt, then infuriated Walter.

At the height of his railing over the Herreras' lack of gratitude, Velma detailed the problems involved in refurbishing the house and finding suitable new tenants. When another letter from Jack Bergan fortuitously arrived in the next day's mail, Walter picked up the phone and called the eight-hundred number. Velma did not know how Jack Bergan had managed the Herreras' eviction, nor did she ever inquire.

She was now joint tenant on a bank account amounting to over two hundred and ninety thousand dollars, and heir to the house and Walter's life insurance and pensions besides. She could not simply take the money from the bank account—even if Walter's friends at the bank did not notify him moments after such a withdrawal, where could she run to that Walter would not find her? No, it would all be hers only when Walter died, and never mind that blood-sucking brother of his.

If only Water would die.

The phrase echoing in her mind, she immediately told herself she meant nothing by it. Over the following days, as the thought further implanted itself, she argued that she was not truly contemplating murder, merely examining the possibility out of pure curiosity. And she continued to repeat this to herself during the months she spent seeking a method, a foolproof plan: she was merely searching out the solution to a difficult and fascinating puzzle, the only interesting thing she'd found to do since coming to this dreary town.

It was no easy matter, she learned, to safely rid oneself of a person. Modern crime detection techniques were too highly sophisticated. And when the person was an ex-sheriff who knew how to protect himself, who had strong ties to current law enforcement, the problem was immeasurably more thorny.

She dismissed the idea of a handgun: how did one go about finding an unregistered weapon and disposing of it properly afterward? Walter of course had a gun—his old service revolver—but the possibility of arranging an accident with that weapon seemed hopeless.

And how did one go about obtaining undetectable or untraceable poison? Stabbing was out of the question; it required expertise as well as a high degree of luck, and made a dreadful mess besides. Other methods—gassing, bludgeoning, pushing Walter from a height, arranging an accident with the car—presented their own problems. What if the result was not death but permanent injury? What could be worse than being condemned to caring for Walter Kennon, invalid, for the rest of her life or his? And if she was caught and convicted of murder, she would undoubtedly go to jail for the rest of her life, if not face a hideous death inhaling cyanide in California's gas chamber.

Given the fact that any method had to be absolutely foolproof, arranging Walter's death by other than natural causes seemed an impossibility. Yet there had to be some way. . . .

IV

As Jessie traversed the circle she had drawn on the real estate map, Kate asked several times to stop. Once she got out of the car to look over a low bluff into a grassy ravine; then to tramp a weed-choked lot; then to scuff a jogging shoe in the dirt of another lot recently cleared of its brush. As daylight faded to gray, she had Jessie stop at Rolling Hills Cemetery.

Jessie stood with Kate on the tar-surfaced road alongside the graveyard, its long green hillside extending all the way down to the fog-shrouded sea perhaps a quarter of a mile away. A hand extended over her eyes as if she were shading them from the sun, Kate looked out over the perfectly sodded graves with their embedded granite markers.

Realizing the memories undoubtedly triggered by this scene, Jessie offered gruffly, "My folks are buried here, you know." She gestured toward a distant green hill. "On the old side where Alice Kennon is. It doesn't have these flat headstones that all look alike." Kate nodded in reply. Jessie reflected that she herself was getting just as cantankerous as Walt Kennon about every change in the world she knew and loved.

Kate lowered herself to a knee and ran a hand over the bent Bermuda grass of the hillside. "Tell me again what Walt was wearing Friday night."

"Gray corduroys, a blue plaid Pendleton shirt."

"A plastic raincoat, you said."

"That too. He arrived in it. A black one."

Kate stood, brushed her hands together to remove the dust of the grass. She walked slowly and for some distance along the hillside, stopping just beyond a white stake to examine a single tire track beside the paved road, any distinguishing features of the track obliterated by the recent rain.

"I have to tell you," Jessie muttered, staring down the smooth, steep hillside, "I considered the notion Velma might've rolled him down this hill and all the way to the ocean, I really did. I even walked it. But the land flattens out down there—" she gestured, "—a good hundred yards at the bottom of the hill. No way she could push or drag him to where the hill drops again. No way in hell."

Kate said, "I'd have considered the exact same idea, Jess."

Her hand once more across her eyes, Kate again surveyed the cemetery, a deepening gray shadow as nightfall approached. Jessie felt a renewed comfort that Kate was here and reviewing every detail of this investigation with her.

"Jess."

Alerted by the tone, Jessie looked sharply at Kate; but she was turned away from her.

"Anne told me once she wanted cremation." The tone was low, distant. "But I buried her, you know. Cremation was what her family wanted too, but they were good enough to leave me alone about it. The thing was, she burned to death. I couldn't bear to burn her again. Can you understand that?"

Jessie managed to find her voice. "I do understand. I do."

"But I think about her all the time there in the ground. And her not wanting to be where she is."

Jessie took Kate's arm. "I think she'd want exactly what you wanted," she said quietly, firmly. "I think she'd understand. I think she wouldn't mind."

Kate turned to Jessie, slid an arm around her waist, walked with Jessie toward the police car.

V

Velma could not remember the precise moment when she made the clear and irrevocable decision to kill Walter, but it was soon after that morning when she waited in the car as Walter paid his weekly visit to Alice's grave. She observed the cemetery custodians rolling a freshly sodded grave, completing the interment process for a funeral held the day before, and she realized then that the true key lay not in foolproof method but in foolproof disposal of the body.

In the days afterward, she deduced a method for ending Walter's life that would leave no evidence behind, deduced the exact circumstances that would allow her to handle more than a hundred and seventy pounds of dead weight. She decided that she would roil the waters of an investigation by withdrawing ten thousand dollars—any lesser amount seeming insufficient to confuse the issue of Walter's disappearance—and stash the money under the flower beds where it could remain until safe to remove; and if it was discovered in the meantime, what did that prove?

To validate her choice of weapon, she made several trips to the library. Then she carefully fashioned her disposable, untraceable bludgeon from sand mixed with heavy steel bolts she found in Walter's tool chest, packing the material into one of Walter's thick wool socks until she was satisfied with the weight and heft. Knowing the act itself would take every ounce of strength, her every fiber of nerve, she waited in a state of feverish dread for ideal conditions.

Each morning she wrenched open the *Courier* to the obituary page. Over a period of the next five weeks there were seven burials at Rolling Hills—but either they were in the old section of the cemetery, or the weather was clear. Twelve times it rained—but there was no funeral.

Each morning as Walter ate his breakfast and prepared for a new day of golf or fishing or gardening, her anxiety grew. It was now March, and the prime rainy season along the Pacific coast was waning. She might very well have to wait until late in the year for the rains to return—six more months at least of living with Walter in this dismal town before she had a likely opportunity.

Then she rose on a Friday morning to gathering black clouds over the ocean and a forecast of rain, occasionally heavy, throughout the day and night. She pulled from her apron pocket a two-day-old obituary:

GRANT R. PAXTON, 68, beloved husband of Margaret Paxton; loving father of John and Edward Paxton; devoted grandfather of Christopher and Julie Paxton.
   Services Friday, Mar. 7, 11:00 am at First Presbyterian Church; interment at Rolling Hills Cemetery.

She had already checked out the Paxton plot; it was located near the cemetery road and held two Paxtons already, with room for four more. Best of all, tonight was poker night; she would not need a pretext to lure Walter to the car at a late hour. Fearful as she was, just as well he would not be home until that late hour.

Pacing the living room, she heard his car pull into the detached garage just before midnight. She flung a raincoat over her shoulders and dashed from the house, her heart thudding, a hand clutching the crude truncheon weighting down her apron pocket.

Walter, his black plastic raincoat shiny with rain, emerged from the car and blinked at her in surprise.

Her voice raspy with strain, she gasped, "I just noticed I lost the diamond in my ring. I'm positive it's in the back of the car."

With a muffled exclamation he turned and yanked open the rear door. Her heart hammering against her ribs, she pushed the raincoat from her shoulders and stepped swiftly up beside him. Gripping the weapon in both hands she swung it behind her to give it the widest possible arc.

He bent down to climb into the car, then started to rise. "The car's been at Phil's station. How—"

She hit him squarely and with all of her strength just along the side and toward the back of the head, exactly where the medical and anatomy books said it was most dangerous to sustain a heavy blow.

There was a single sound from him, a grunted expulsion; then he pitched forward onto the back seat.

She stared, appalled at the concavity in his head, the gray matted hair welling with blood. What had she done wrong? There shouldn't be any blood—there couldn't be any stains on the car's upholstery. Panic-stricken, she stuffed the weapon into her apron pocket, hastily untied the apron and climbed over Walter's back to roughly, tightly bind his head.

She felt for the pulse in his wrist, his neck, as the books had said, as she'd practiced on herself. A second blow would not be necessary; there was no pulse. And she could see that the apron had staunched any flow of blood. Calmer now, she climbed out of the car and went around to the other door. Gripping his shoulders, she pulled and tugged at him, sliding him across the seat on his slick raincoat until he was fully in the car. She closed both doors and retrieved her raincoat, and prepared for the rest of what needed to be done.

VI

Hands in the back pockets of her jeans, Kate stared out the huge windows of Jessie's living room, across the redwood deck at the fog-shrouded lights strung out along the ocean shoreline. As Barbra Streisand sang from Jessie's tape player, Kate prowled the room, looking over the record and tape collection, the bookshelves, poking at the fire, looking at the books again.

"Woman, what's bugging you?" Jessie growled. "Sit down and relax. You're making Damon nervous." The

marmalade-colored cat in her lap was stirring, its ears
pricked.

Kate obediently lowered herself into the armchair beside
the fire, picked up her scotch. "You sure I can't get you
something, Jess?" She gestured to the wicker wine rack
against the dining room wall. "You've got some nice reds
over there."

Jessie shook her head. "Haven't had a thing to drink
since this all began. It's enough trouble as it is to keep my
head clear. I'm so tired, a glass of wine would put me out
like a light."

"How about some coffee?" Kate's tone was solicitous.
"Be glad to make it for you."

"Nope, that'll keep me wide awake and I hope to sleep a
few hours tonight." She looked sharply at Kate, who was
fidgeting with her scotch. She reiterated, "What's bugging
you, woman?"

"Jess . . ." Kate put the scotch down on her coaster.

It was the same quiet use of her name as at the cemetery,
and Jessie watched her uneasily.

"There was a funeral last week at Rolling Hills
Cemetery," Kate said. It was a statement, not a question.

"Probably," Jessie answered, a prickling sensation along
the back of her neck. "There's usually about one a week. I
know for sure they buried Grant Paxton there. He ran
Seacliff Reality. I knew him to say hello to."

"He was buried last Friday," Kate stated.

Jessie stared at her. "I don't know about that, but I can
check it in a second."

She pulled herself out of her leather recliner and moved
to the stack of papers on the brick hearth. "I haven't looked
at a newspaper in days. . . ." She sorted through the stack
until she found last Friday's *Courier*, opened it to the
obituary page.

Jessie dropped the paper back onto the stack, sat down
on the hearth and looked up at Kate. Her hands, all of her
flesh was cold. "Like you said, Paxton was buried Friday.
What are you telling me, Kate?"

Kate closed her eyes. "I'm sorry, Jess. Your gut feeling
about Walter . . . is right."

Jessie rubbed her arms, edged closer to the fire. "I knew it." But still she had hoped. . . .

"I'm sorry, Jess," Kate repeated.

"It's better I know. Just tell me how this was done."

VII

Driving slowly through the sheeting windblown rain, Velma pulled onto the road above Rolling Hills Cemetery and extinguished the car lights. The night was opaque in its blackness; and she drifted the car along until the fourth white roadside marker loomed by her side window. She pulled carefully over onto the grassy side of the road just beyond the marker and turned off the engine. She stripped off her raincoat; it would be useless in this downpour, and encumbering. She got out, opened the rear door of the Toyota.

Pulling, tugging Walter by his shoulders, her foot braced against the side of the car, she inched him across the seat until his head emerged from the car and struck the grass. Quickly she climbed into the car behind him and pushed his legs until he pitched fully out.

She closed the car doors, got the shovel out of the trunk. Again she pulled and tugged at Walter until he lay sideways on the hill. Bracing herself once more, she gave his body a mighty shove. He tumbled down the slope, his head flopping; she lost sight of him in the rain-filled blackness.

Carrying the shovel, wiping the pelting rain from her eyes, she staggered down the steep hill and nearly stumbled over his body. She slid the shovel down the hill, knowing she could find it later, then pushed Walter, rolling him over and over in the spongy Bermuda grass, the apron coming off his head.

Standing between his legs as if she were pulling a plow, she dragged him farther, the wet slippery grass and Walter's slick plastic raincoat enabling her to maneuver him, as she had judged they would. She and her mother had once used a similar method—a quilt under a huge, heavy chest to move it down into the basement. But she had been so much younger then. . . .

Rain streaming from her hair into her blind eyes, she moaned with her straining effort. Would she ever get there?

Then she tripped over the edge of the tarpaulin and pitched headlong onto the mound of the newly dug Paxton grave.

She sat on the tarpaulin and rested a few moments, her chest heaving. Then she climbed to her feet and used her tiny flashlight to locate the shovel as well as the apron that had come off Walter's head. She removed the rock-weighted tarpaulin, then the freshly laid strips of sod over Grant Paxton's grave, placing the strips with care on the tarpaulin to keep them intact.

Frenziedly, she began to dig, throwing shovel after shovel of the loose dirt onto the tarpaulin; the earth was becoming heavier as the teeming rain soaked it. When she reached a depth of several feet, she turned quickly to Walter.

Gritting her teeth, her arms quivering with the effort, she tugged and maneuvered him to the edge of the grave. Then gave him one final push. He thudded into the grave, face down. She threw in the apron, the weapon still in its pocket, and Walter's car keys.

She shoveled the earth back, grunting with the heaviness of each shovelful, her entire body trembling with this final exertion, and reshaped the mass of it into a mound, the surface a rapidly smoothing mud. Then she lay the strips of sod back and reset the tarpaulin. And the rocks weighting the corners of the tarpaulin. Finally, she shook the muddy earth from the shovel and wiped it on grass.

Her legs giving way, her limbs jerking, she collapsed on the hillside in an agony of exhaustion, thinking she might die here herself. The rain picked up in fury, pelting her mercilessly, and she lay unmoving, allowing it to slash the mud from her hands, her feet and legs, her clothes, her face.

As strength seeped back into her, she reviewed her next steps—no time now to make the slightest mistake. She would drive home, change into dry clothes. Destroy Walter's handwritten will in the fireplace and pulverize the ashes.

Abruptly she sat up. She had already made a mistake. The key to the desk was on Walter's keychain; she had buried it along with Walter. She lay back down again. It wasn't that much of a mistake. A sturdy kitchen knife would be sufficient to spring the desk drawer. After taking this much risk she *definitely* would not share any of her gains with anyone. It was now nearly one o'clock; at two she would call the Sheriff's office and report Walter missing, and then it would all be finished.

When her limbs finally ceased their trembling, she struggled to her feet, switched on the small flashlight, and inspected her handiwork. The Paxton grave looked untouched, the thundering rain continuing to wash away all traces of her presence. Even the shovel had been scoured clean of its evidence. Finally she summoned strength for the climb up the hill to the car, and to freedom. She had done it. And no one could possibly guess how.

VIII

Jessie moved away from the fire. She was warm, heated by anger, her mind seething with the image of the false grief on Velma Kennon's face that Saturday morning, scant hours after Velma had ruthlessly killed her own husband and Jessie's irreplaceable friend.

"I'm sorry," Kate said softly. "There was no good or gentle way to tell you any of this."

No one, Jessie thought, could have been more gentle than Kate. Not even Irene would be as good with her as this woman, with whom she shared an alien profession whose daily stock in trade was violence, who had herself been touched by the annihilating hand of death.

Kate said, "Of course you won't know if I'm right until . . ."

"I know it now." Jessie took a deep breath. "Everything you've theorized makes perfect sense. It does. To do what she did and then put him in someone else's grave—" she hissed, "It's *obscene*."

Kate murmured, "Maybe I can get you some of that wine now?"

Jessie shook her head. She walked over to Kate, sat down on the ottoman in front of her armchair. "I can't imagine how you figured this out."

"Anne told me," Kate said.

Jessie gaped at her.

"And then you told me the rest. The answers all came at Rolling Hills." Kate's eyes were fixed unseeingly on the fire; her voice was remote. "Looking over that place, I was remembering the day after Anne was buried. I drove out to the cemetery very early that next morning. I wanted to be with her. . . . I wanted to dig with my bare hands till I could be in there with her."

Jessie, her eyes stinging, kept her silence. Kate's renewed anguish over Anne was her fault. In sharing Jessie's sorrow, Kate had ripped the scar tissue from her own grief.

Kate's voice strengthened. "But you're the one who's responsible for solving this crime. How many investigating officers would have thought to check that Union Oil sticker? Velma Kennon would have gotten away with murder except for you. And your notion about Velma rolling him down the hill and all the way to the ocean—when I realized she wouldn't have to roll him far at all, it came together then, how a new grave as soon as it's rolled and sodded looks just like any other grave. And how Velma could use the rain, the slope of the cemetery and its bent Bermuda grass, Walt's slippery raincoat—" Fixing her somber eyes on Jessie, Kate shrugged. "And aside from all that, it seems after thirteen years in the cop business I'm beginning to think right along with the criminals."

Jessie sighed. She said softly, "You'd best get on to bed, Kate. Much as I want to, I can't lock Velma up tonight—not a thing to be done till morning and I get the search warrant to go in and get Walt. You've got only these few days of vacation; I want you out of here bright and early—"

"I'll stay up with you," Kate said firmly.

Jessie shook her head. "It's all on my shoulders now, Kate. I'd like to be alone with my thoughts."

Kate said quietly, "I do understand that, Jess."

With Kate settled in the guest bedroom, Jessie sat in her armchair and stared into the fire. But she did not yet think of Walt Kennon, or begin to mourn him; there was time enough for that. Instead she thought about Kate Delafield on vacation, making her solitary, lonely way up the California coast.

IX

The next morning, Velma again looked at the *Courier*'s obituary page. Margaret Paxton would be buried today next to her dead husband—and Velma's. Velma swallowed the last of her tea and dismissed a brief impulse to attend. That

would be foolish, would only arouse comment, if not
suspicion. She had not realized that the bond of friendship
between Walter Kennon and Jessie Graham ran as deep as it
did—and she could not be too careful in these final days of
the sheriff's investigation.

Velma looked up to see a patrol car coming up the block
toward her house. Odd. This was out of pattern—another
patrol car had already performed its half-hourly surveillance
routine only fifteen minutes ago.

Then the patrol car was joined by Jessie Graham's car
with its gold sheriff's insignia. With a surge of alarm, Velma
watched both cars turn into her driveway as yet another
police car came from the opposite direction to join them,
screeching to a stop in front of the house.

Feeling the blood drain from her face, Velma watched
Jessie Graham climb out of her car and adjust the gunbelt
over her dark brown trousers. The sheriff reached into her
car to retrieve some sort of plastic sack; then marched
toward the house at a purposeful pace, flanked by three
deputies who drew their weapons as they approached the
door.

What could this be? What had gone wrong? She had
made no mistakes, *nothing* had gone wrong, there was no
way on earth Jessie Graham could know *anything*.

Harassment, she decided. A last-ditch, desperation
attempt to panic her, stampede her into making a mistake.
Seeing the neighbors gather on their lawns and sidewalks to
observe, Velma angrily threw open her front door. "What's
the meaning of this . . . *circus?*"

"You're under arrest, Velma." The words were said with
barely controlled rage; the dark eyes were implacably cold.

Holding the plastic sack by a corner, Sheriff Jessie
Graham held it up to Velma's eyes.

A hand at her throat as if cyanide fumes were already
choking her, Velma stared at her dirty, blood-stained apron.

THE SACRIFICE

Kate Downey

The child's body was found Sunday morning around seven-thirty. A man walking his dog in a wooded culvert between Valley Road and Wellborn Creek had discovered her, drawn to the site by the animal's persistent whimpering and scratching. It was an isolated spot, although not far from the road. The grave, hidden between two fir trees, was disguised by their shadow and hard to see from a distance. Even up close, a thin blanket of drifting autumn leaves shrouded and concealed it. If the dog had not discovered it, the child's shallow last resting place might have remained undisturbed for weeks.

She lay swaddled in plastic, and through the cloudy wrappings bruises could be seen on her small, naked body. Later, the medical examiner would discover that besides the beating, she had been raped and strangled.

She was seven years old.

♦

Sheriff Paul Rabbitt hated the autopsy room with its gleaming, heartless tile and stainless steel, the cruel bright instruments, the remorseless thoroughness of the surgeon. Above all he hated the smells, at once clinical and morbid, that assaulted him. But he had never hated it more than when he entered it to witness the autopsy on little Lynn Ann Ryerson. He went home immediately afterward. There was still time to go into the office, but he couldn't endure the miasma of formaldehyde and death that encircled him like a noxious halo. He had to take a shower, change his clothes.

In the shower he fiercely scrubbed himself until his skin turned red. He washed his hair twice. He put on a clean pair of sweats, since it was now late enough to justify not going back to the office. He would call in later.

He fixed himself a sandwich and ate it mechanically. He started to hunt for a pack of cigarettes before he remembered, for possibly the thousandth time in the past two days, that he had given up smoking three months ago. It was the longest he'd gone without a cigarette since he was fifteen. Nervously he passed the long fingers of his big hands through his dark brown hair, disheveling the still-damp waves, and cursed his stalwart abstinence.

He took a bottle of Heineken out of the refrigerator as a poor substitute and went into the living room. He switched on the TV and caught the early news. A smiling image of Lynn Ann Ryerson in a party dress was displayed on the screen. In voiceover the anchorwoman described how the Mountain Glen Sheriff's Department, with the help of the state police, was combing the Catskills area for clues to the identity of her killer, so far without success. Switch to a videotape of the child's hysterically weeping mother.

Rabbitt hit the remote and the screen went dark. He felt horribly close to crying himself. He upended the beer bottle, gulping the contents, and got up for another one. At least he had plenty of that in the house.

Now in his mid-forties, he had been a widower for five years. He lived alone. Mostly he didn't mind. Often he welcomed the solitude. But today it held no peace for him. Today he missed his wife with an aching intensity he hadn't felt for years. Only her presence might have comforted him. He knew nothing else could.

He had been the one to break the news to Dolores Ryerson. She had stared at him with eyes swollen and red from the weeping she had already done since the little girl had disappeared three days before. Incoherent with grief, she had been unable to tell him anything helpful, including the whereabouts of her husband, who had left home the day after the child's disappearance and not returned since.

Why Ryerson had gone at such a time, when presumably he and his wife needed each other the most, where he was, or when he would be back were all vital questions. Yet Rabbitt found those answers elusive. Karl Ryerson wasn't the kind of man to run away from trouble. He was an auto mechanic who owned his own service station, and he had a county-wide reputation for competence, honesty—and dependability. He was deeply religious. Both the Ryersons were—in the sheriff's opinion, to a fault. His disappearance didn't make a lot of sense to Rabbitt.

Unless, of course, Ryerson had killed his daughter.

The phone rang. Rabbitt put aside his half finished beer and answered it. It was Dr. Kimberly Krieger, the medical examiner who had autopsied Lynn Ann.

"Just wanted to let you know my prelim on the Ryerson girl will be on your desk late tomorrow morning."

"Good, Kim. Thanks." He paused, knowing there would be more or she would not have bothered to call.

"Karl Ryerson turn up yet?" Dr. Krieger asked.

"Not yet," Rabbitt told her.

"It looks bad for him, Paul," she said, her voice somber.

"You think he did it?"

"So do you," she countered.

Rabbitt was silent. They both knew it was an ugly fact that child molesters were rarely strangers to their victims. Most were relatives, close family friends, even parents. Just the same, he hated to acknowledge it.

Dr. Krieger didn't push it. "I sent a semen sample and a blood sample from the girl to the lab for DNA fingerprinting," she continued. "That'll at least tell us if she was related to the man who raped her."

"But that'll only tell us if it *could* have been her father. And it still won't tell us who killed her," Rabbitt said.

"No," she agreed. "It won't do that." Then she added, "By the way, strangulation wasn't the cause of death."

"What?" he protested. "But the marks, Kim."

"Oh, yeah, yeah," Dr. Krieger cut in. "She was certainly choked. But she wasn't strangled to death. And she didn't die of internal injuries, either."

"What, then?" he demanded.

"She was smothered." There was a pause. "Catch this son of a bitch, Paul," Dr. Krieger urged. "And when you do, I hope he gives you an excuse to shoot him." Then she hung up.

Her words were an uncomfortable echo of Rabbitt's own thoughts.

Spurred into action by her revelations, Rabbitt dialed his office number. Deputy Miller answered.

"Lee? Anything on the Ryerson case?" Rabbitt asked, brusqueness reflecting his sense of urgency. Miller had a passion for forensics. If there were any physical traces to be found, he would ferret them out.

Miller gave him a brief rundown. There had been at least ten new phone calls added to the hundred they had already received, with a bewildering variety of leads, hints, and obvious lies. These were all being checked out. Ryerson was still missing. Deputy Becker had Ryerson's service station— presently closed—under surveillance, but there was no sign of life there as yet.

"Sheriff, one more thing," Miller said. "I found prints on the plastic sheeting that was around the kid's body." The deputy could not keep the triumph from his voice. "They were on one of the corners. Thumb on one side, three fingers on the other. Fingers are a little smudged, but the thumb's nice and clear."

"Good work, Lee," Rabbitt commended, meaning it. "Now all we've got to find out is who those prints belong to. Get Maguire on it and call me immediately if anything else turns up." Then the sheriff added, "And we've got to find Ryerson." He hung up.

He sat holding the portable phone in his hand, playing idly with the antenna. If whoever cut the plastic didn't bother to wear gloves, he must've cut it for something else and had it handy when he needed it. A lot of people used that type of plastic sheeting for makeshift storm windows. The basement windows of the Ryerson house had been covered with it. But so were others in the district.

His brooding was broken by the sound of a vehicle approaching, pulling into his driveway. Cursing under his breath, Rabbitt went to the window and peered through the blind. He was not in the mood to socialize.

♦

The light over the garage revealed a blue Ford pickup. He recognized it at once. The owner was Michael Shay, the most prominent member of the New Church of the Eternal Jerusalem, the religious sect—cult, the sheriff considered it— to which the Ryersons belonged. It was a tight-knit group whose members subscribed to fundamentalist Judeo-Christian beliefs. Rabbitt thought the group was extreme, and he kept a wary eye on their activities. He had begun inquiries into the backgrounds of its members after Lynn Ann's disappearance.

Rabbitt had already interviewed Shay, who was also a neighbor of the Ryersons. Intrigued by this unexpected visit, the sheriff hurried to the door. The doorbell was still chiming when he opened it.

Brother Michael—the form of address he preferred—was in his early forties. He was of average height and compact build, with thick, straight black hair and a well-trimmed full beard. Both his hair and beard were attractively streaked with gray. He greeted the sheriff and apologized in his soft-spoken way for the intrusion.

Rabbitt nodded a curt greeting and gestured him in. Shay followed him into the living room and sat down on the sofa. Rabbitt sat in the recliner opposite him. His visitor looked ill at ease, conscious that he was intruding.

Feeling under no obligation to play host, the sheriff waited for Brother Michael to state his business. Shay began by explaining that he had been on his way home from visiting Dolores Ryerson, having spent the evening in prayer with her, and realized that he was passing the sheriff's house.

"I just had to see if there was anything I could do to help." With a self-deprecating smile, Shay spread his hands in a gesture almost benedictory.

"What kind of help did you have in mind?" Rabbitt asked, interested to know where Shay was leading.

"Karl is still missing, isn't he?" Brother Michael asked, his voice scarcely above a whisper.

Rabbitt side-stepped the question by asking another. "When did you last see him or talk to him?"

"The day after his daughter disappeared. He came to my house," Brother Michael explained. "In the New Church we all do our best to support each other. He was in a terrible state over what happened to poor little Lynn Ann." He paused and his face assumed an expression of sad, reflection. He lowered his head for a moment, as if in prayer, then looking up at the sheriff, continued. "I tried to help him. I knew he needed to express his grief, so I listened to him for a while. But nothing I could say helped." He spread his hand in a gesture of futility. "I tried to get him to pray with me, but he wouldn't." He shook his head. "Maybe he couldn't. I remember thinking at the time, that it was more like despair than grief that he was feeling. Actually, he frightened me. He seemed so depressed. I was worried about him."

Rabbitt digested this narrative, privately wondering how anyone could be sufficiently blinded by religious fervor to turn to Brother Michael for consolation. Shay's words, gestures, tone, facial expression were all correct, the perfect semblance of a concerned clergyman. But Rabbitt sensed no real feeling behind the outward appearance. He saw no compassion in Shay's eyes.

Rabbitt leaned forward. "Did he tell you anything that might be relevant to Lynn Ann's death?" His voice was stern.

Shay hesitated, then shook his head vigorously. "No, no. He didn't *say* anything like that."

Impatient to get at the truth, Rabbitt fought the urge to grab Shay and shake it out of him. "Just what are you trying to say?" he demanded.

"He couldn't live with the guilt of what he did to his own daughter." Brother Michael seemed to force the words out, reluctant to give them breath.

The words jolted the sheriff. "You know this for a fact? He told you this?"

"No, he didn't," Brother Michael insisted. "But he was really crazy that night. As I said, desperate. I can put two and two together, sheriff."

"Yeah," Rabbitt said sourly. He felt sick again. He forced himself to ask one more question. "Do you have any idea where he is?"

Brother Michael rose, anxious now to leave. "I'm afraid I don't."

Silence. It was obvious that Shay would say nothing more. He turned to go. The sheriff followed him to the door.

"Good night, Brother Paul," Shay said.

"Good night," Rabbitt responded. He stood in the doorway watching Michael Shay as he climbed into his pickup and drove away.

He went back inside and sat nursing his beer. He considered the facts he had in the case. Someone had assaulted Lynn Ann. Beaten her. Choked her. Raped her. Then smothered her—to keep her from screaming? And it was beginning to seem certain that that someone was her now-missing father. Shay seemed sure that it was. So did Kim Krieger.

Ryerson's disappearance, the sheriff concluded, was becoming more and more ominous. Rabbitt was all too well acquainted with the more despicable aspects of human nature. During his fifteen years in law enforcement he had encountered most of them. Ryerson now seemed to be the prime suspect, and even his own pastor, Brother Shay, appeared unwilling to protect his congregant, certain that he was guilty.

He pictured Karl, a tall, thin man whose once-ginger hair, grayed to the color of sand, stood out from his head in thin wisps like spun glass. His wide, pale-blue gaze was habitually startled, and the expression in his eyes marked him as both puzzled and saddened by the inequities of life. Had these inequities led him to kill his daughter?

He needed to find Ryerson. Karl's absence was like a black hole sucking in everything surrounding it. Rabbitt knew that until he had solved the mystery of Ryerson's disappearance he would never discover the truth of Lynn Ann's death. And he owed it to the dead child to find her killer—even, or maybe especially, if it was her own father.

Maybe if he checked out the service station one more time Rabbitt might see something they had missed before, something that might give a clue to the man's whereabouts. He didn't bother changing his clothes. He strapped on his revolver and threw on a jacket. The day had been chilly; the night would be cold. Ryerson's Quality Service Station wasn't far, about a twenty-minute drive. Rabbitt radioed Becker that he was on his way and to maintain his surveillance.

He pulled up in front of the closed garage bay doors. If Karl Ryerson was there, the sheriff wanted him to know he had company.

Rabbitt got out of his car and drew his gun. Scarcely breathing, he walked with slow caution around the building, seeing nothing but worn tires and a mangled Dodge van up on blocks. There was an uncanny stillness about the place that spooked him. The hairs on his neck and arms bristled in response.

He came around to the front of the shop. There was a sign on it that read "Closed," as it had every day since Lynn Ann had disappeared. The front door was unlocked. This had not been the case when Rabbitt had been there three days ago after Karl had first gone missing. Rabbitt glanced toward Becker's place of concealment and gestured for him. Hoping his deputy would actually follow him, he entered the shop.

There was no one inside.

The door that led to the work area was closed. Rabbitt opened it. The close atmosphere of the garage was permeated by a stench that combined motor oil, car exhaust, and something else that made his stomach heave. With difficulty he kept from being sick. He fumbled for the switch beside the bay doors, found it and sent them rumbling upward, letting in the clean night air. He could see Becker approaching at a dog trot.

He switched on the lights.

There was only one car inside, a gray Ford Escort, its windows rolled down. Rabbitt didn't remember seeing it there before. He moved closer. Ryerson sat behind the steering wheel. His head was thrown back, his mouth slack, his eyes open and staring. His normally pallid skin was flushed, but nevertheless there was no doubt that he was dead.

◆

"I won't call it suicide." Dr. Krieger's voice was firm. She was a short, fifty-something woman with uncompromisingly gray hair, and she regarded pity for the victims of violent death as a snare to be avoided. Pity could blunt the edge of her intellect, and she needed to keep her head clear. But in the unyielding glare of the morgue lights, her set face reflected both her fatigue and her dejection, the by-products of too much senseless death. Sometimes she found it was impossible to keep her emotions at bay.

Beside her stood Rabbitt, and between them, on a metal table, lay the naked, sheet-draped body of Ryerson.

"Oh, shit," he muttered, looking down at the corpse. Then his gaze shifted to the woman beside him. He raised a speculative eyebrow. "What *would* you call it?"

She did not answer immediately. "Give me a hand, will you?" she requested.

Concealing his distaste, Rabbitt helped Dr. Krieger raise the corpse to a sitting position. He held it firm while she pointed to a spot at the base of the skull.

"He was hit here hard enough to fracture his skull. You can feel it." She looked at Rabbitt expectantly, but he shook his head, having no desire to verify her words. "No external bleeding," she added. "Didn't break the skin."

Gently they let the body back down.

"The blow to the head didn't kill him," she continued. "He wasn't dead when the car engine was turned on. He died from carbon monoxide poisoning." She drew the concealing sheet back into place. "You said that wasn't his car he was found in?"

Rabbitt nodded assent.

"Somebody drove him to the station, then," she added. "I don't see him getting there under his own steam."

"Murder," the sheriff said glumly. "How long has he been dead?"

"I can't say for sure. Day and a half, maybe two."

It was after midnight. Dr. Krieger turned off the lights, and she and Rabbitt left. In the hall she paused, took off her glasses and rubbed her eyes. "At least now we'll be able to get a definite tissue match. We'll know for sure if Karl was the rapist," she said, as if that were a consolation.

"Yeah," he said, with no enthusiasm. "But it still won't tell us who killed her. And it sure won't tell us who killed him."

"The missus?" Dr. Krieger suggested. "She knew he was guilty right from the start, so she killed him. I've never met her. Could she possibly have moved him?"

Rabbitt shook his head. "No way. She's a little thing. Of course," he added, "she might have had help."

"I've been thinking, Paul," Dr. Krieger said as they waited by the elevator. "Those New Church people keep to themselves. Even most of Ryerson's customers were New Church people. If it wasn't Karl, it had to be someone from the Church. That kid didn't know anyone else."

The elevator arrived.

"Don't think I haven't thought of that," he told her as they stepped onto the car. "They're being checked out."

They rode up to the main level in silence. At the exit, they paused. Dr. Krieger fished her car keys from her purse, then looked up at Rabbitt. "Maybe the wife couldn't have carried Karl's body, but she could have carried Lynn Ann's," she said.

"That she could," he agreed, heavy-hearted. Dolores Ryerson as the murderer of her daughter was a picture he didn't like, but he couldn't deny its possibility.

They went outside. "See you tomorrow for this one?" Dr. Krieger asked through a barely suppressed yawn.

Rabbitt knew she meant the autopsy. He nodded. He had gotten little enough sleep the night before, and he'd be lucky if he got any that night. There was still one thing he had to do. It had been hard enough telling Mrs. Ryerson that her daughter's body had been found. But now he had to tell her that her husband, too, had been murdered. And he would have to watch her face for signs of guilt.

Dolores Ryerson accepted the news blank-faced, with seeming stoicism. Was it just that she was already too benumbed with grief to fully register the news? Or did her lack of outward reaction conceal her own sin? He had left reluctantly, feeling helpless, powerless to either comfort or condemn her.

When Rabbitt finally got home, he was too keyed up and too depressed to sleep. In the kitchen, he dropped a couple of ice cubes into a tumbler and poured a generous amount of Scotch over them. He drank it fast, then took the nearly full bottle into the living room. He threw his long frame into his lounge chair and leaned back, his relaxed posture belying his churning mind. Tomorrow he would begin a second and more extensive round of interviews with the Ryerson's friends and acquaintances. And Dolores Ryerson.

♦

The next morning, groggy from too little sleep and too much alcohol, Rabbitt went into the office. Lee Miller was there. He had been busy all night going over the victim's clothing, painfully sifting for any incriminating minutiae they might contain. Persistent and lucky, he had extracted from among the fibers at the left side seam of Karl's red wool sweater three short, coarse hairs—two black, one white. They couldn't have belonged to the red-headed Karl. Miller had also compared Karl's fingerprints to those found on the plastic. They were not a match.

Rabbitt was gratified, though his satisfaction at the news only went so far. Three hairs was a thin thread on which to hang much hope. But as he left the office to attend the autopsy on Ryerson, in his mind's eye he saw the face of Michael Shay, his black hair and beard attractively streaked with gray.

As Rabbitt stood by the table in the autopsy room watching Dr. Krieger's systematic butchery, he thought about Michael Shay's visit the evening before. Shay, he realized, had played him for a sucker. With his phony concerned-man-of-God act he had carefully planted the idea of Ryerson's suicidal depression and probable guilt.

Rabbitt's anger and disgust over Lynn Ann's rape and murder, his horror at Ryerson's assumed culpability, and above all his pity for Dolores Ryerson all blended and turned into blind fury at Michael Shay. The stupid bastard. Did Shay really think he would get away with it? One way or another, Rabbitt was determined that he wouldn't.

It was close to four o'clock, and Dr. Krieger was just finishing the autopsy when Rabbitt's beeper sounded. He

called the office. There was news, Miller reported. Shay's
fingerprints were a match for the prints on the plastic.
Furthermore, he had an unsavory past. Deputy Maguire had
uncovered three arrests over the past twelve years—one for
rape, one for assault and battery, and one for child abuse.
The first two charges had been dropped. Apparently, there
had been insufficient evidence to try him on the other charge.

It was time, Rabbitt decided, to have a little heart-to-
heart with Brother Michael Shay. He left immediately for
Shay's house.

His right hand resting on the .38 at his hip, Rabbitt
raised his left and pounded on the door. Shay opened it. He
must have only just gotten home from work. An electrician,
he was still dressed in jeans, work shirt, and boots.

"Good evening, Sheriff," he said, his face an unreadable
mask.

"I've got a few questions for you, Reverend Shay," the
sheriff said without ceremony.

Looking apprehensive now, Shay let him in and ushered
him into the kitchen. Shay sat down at the kitchen table.
Rabbitt followed suit.

The sheriff got right to the point. "Karl Ryerson's been
found. He's dead."

"I was afraid he would do something like that," Shay
began. "He was so—" he trailed off.

"Depressed." Rabbitt finished the sentence.

"Yes," Shay agreed.

"He didn't kill himself, Shay. Somebody did it for him.
He was murdered."

That final lurid word echoed in the absolute silence that
followed. "Murdered?" Shay looked confused, as if he didn't
understand what he had heard. "Who did it?" he stammered.

"The same man who raped and murdered Lynn Ann."
Now face to face with Shay, Rabbitt could barely control
himself.

Brother Michael turned pale. "How can you know
that?" he asked.

Rabbitt sprang to his feet. In three steps he was around
the table. Shay gave a cry of alarm as the sheriff grabbed him
by the shirt front and dragged him to his feet. His chair
crashed to the floor behind him.

"You dumb-ass piece of shit," Rabbitt snarled, shaking the terrified Shay. He shoved him backward against the wall. Shay gave a cry of pain and fear as his head hit the wall.

Rabbitt was on him again, pinning him immobile where he stood. "Did you really think you could get away with it?" Somewhere behind the wall of his own hot killing fury, Rabbitt knew he should stop, knew he should back off. But he didn't want to. Not yet. Not yet.

Shay struggled. "I didn't do anything. I didn't kill anyone," he gasped.

"I'm going to prove you did," Rabbitt hissed, his face only inches from the struggling man. "You'd better really pray, now."

Shay began to sob. Rabbitt, dragging him away from the wall and spinning him around, knocked him to the floor with a vicious punch in the face. Shay cowered face down. Rabbitt dragged him up and hit him again. He didn't fall this time, but staggered backward and half-stumbled, half-ran into the hallway.

Rabbitt was after him. As Shay fumbled to open the door, the sheriff drew his gun.

"Freeze," he ordered.

Shay either didn't hear or couldn't stop himself. He pulled the door open. Rabbitt grabbed him by the back of his collar and pulled him away from the door. Shay stumbled and fell on the floor. He looked up and froze as he saw the gun pointing down at him.

"No," he gasped. "No." Then he began to cry. "I didn't mean it," he sobbed. "I didn't mean to hurt her."

"Shut up," Rabbitt ordered. He glanced quickly over his shoulder. Becker and Miller were outside, as he had ordered them before. Becker was still in the car, but Miller was running up the walk; Rabbitt registered his look of alarm.

Shay was still babbling out a disjointed confession. "And Karl. It was his fault. He came after me. I tried to tell him I didn't mean to hurt her."

Rabbitt knelt beside the terrified man. "I told you once to shut up. You say one more word and I'll kill you."

Miller was in the doorway. "Paul, you need help? He resisting?" he demanded. Rabbitt looked up. Miller fell silent.

"Help me," Shay pleaded.

"Yeah," Rabbitt said. "He's resisting." He remembered Kim Krieger's words, "When you find him, I hope he gives you an excuse to shoot him."

Miller understood the look on the sheriff's face. He put out a hand. "Don't, Paul," he cautioned.

Rabbitt stood up and looked back down at Shay. "You're under arrest," he said. "For the murders of Lynn Ann Ryerson and Karl Ryerson." Then he turned back to Miller.

"Read him his rights, Deputy." Miller obliged. As the deputy helped the terrified Shay to his feet and cuffed him, Rabbitt said to him, "Now, Reverend, you can talk all you want."

Back in his car, Rabbitt closed his eyes, exhausted. He was shaking and sick with excess adrenalin and blood lust, his body clammy with sweat. He knew he had come close to killing Michael Shay. And he knew, with despair, that he wished he had.

An Expatriate Death

Barbara Wilson

It wasn't the first thing I was supposed to notice about the charming colonial Mexican town of San Andreas, but I did, at the beginning and ever after. When I look back on the whole experience, it's the memory of the high stucco walls and the glass shards embedded in them that comes too readily to mind. Not every house in San Andreas had these kinds of outer walls, of course—the Indian houses didn't have them, nor those of most of the Mexicans. The walls were mainly to protect the white expatriates, the wealthy ones, those who had moved to San Andreas because it was so picturesque. You had to admit that the broken glass stuck along the tops of the walls was probably more picturesque than barbed wire.

Eleanor Harrington, the woman who was renting me and Lucy her house for a week, had walls like these, but she was so used to them that she didn't bother to comment as she unlocked the heavy wooden outer door and led us through a patio brimming with bright pots of flowering succulents. Eleanor Harrington was in her early fifties and had pinkish-blond hair, bouffant with thin bangs, milky blue eyes, and a face that was paler than her neck and arms. She wore a cotton embroidered smock, sleeveless and low-necked, over her stretch pants, and her tanned arms were ringed up to the elbow with wide silver bracelets. She'd lived in San Andreas for thirty years, she told us, and had bought this old colonial mansion and had it restored inside and out.

"I really shouldn't be charging you rent at all," she said with the nervous laugh that women often use when they discuss money. "It's really more of a favor to me to have someone here while I go off to see my son in Houston. It's something I do every year, not that I enjoy it much—his wife, you see. . . . But I try never to leave my house unattended, it wouldn't be safe."

In spite of us doing her a favor, she was quick enough to take the check that Lucy held out. "Splendid," she said. "What luck that Georgia mentioned you were looking for a place." She glanced at Lucy, and said, "And did she tell me you were a doctor, Ms. Hernandez?"

"Yes," said Lucy.

"Well, I'm sure you'll enjoy yourself *enormously* here," said Eleanor. "It's meant so much to me to be in San Andreas as long as I have. Of course it's changed a great deal, not always for the better, but it's always had a feeling of home to me. There's so much to do culturally. You must look at our little English language newspaper and see what's going on. There are performances, readings; perhaps you might take a yoga class one day, or even Spanish. You, of course, speak Spanish, Ms. Hernandez . . . where did your parents come from?"

Not smiling back, Lucy said, "San Francisco. San Francisco, California."

Lucy had just spent three months on the Mexican border to Guatemala, working in a refugee camp in a clinic there for mothers and babies. She was on her way back to her job in Oakland, but hearing that I was also planning to pass through Mexico to a conference in Costa Rica, persuaded me to take a brief holiday with her. An acquaintance of hers, a painter, had raved about San Andreas, and had, in the end, come up with a place for us to rent.

Although I had known Lucy for many years and saw her as frequently as I could, I was struck by the change in her. Her light brown skin was matte and dusty-looking, and her hair, which she usually kept very short, was dry and bushy. She was painfully thin as well.

"I'm just tired," she said, after Eleanor had driven off in her red Toyota for the airport in Mexico City, and we were left alone in the living room of the house, with its terra-cotta tiled floor, rugs, and shuttered windows. There were weavings on the couches and bright embroideries on the walls, along with black pottery and the well-known Oaxaca wooden carvings of dogs and other animals, fancifully painted. Some of Eleanor's own sculptures stood among the folk art; they were bronze figures, in the manner of Degas, of Indians, particularly women, often seated, as if at the marketplace.

"We'll put these away while we're here," said Lucy. It was not a question.

And then she went upstairs for a nap although it was only ten in the morning.

♦

I let myself out the locked street door ("Always remember to lock up," were Eleanor's parting words) and went for a walk. Although I'd been in Mexico City a number of times and had explored the southern parts of the country around Oaxaca and the Yucatan, I'd never been in any of the old colonial cities that had been built by the Spanish in the silver-mining days of the seventeenth and eighteenth centuries. There were cobbled streets, pastel and white-painted buildings with thick walls, and inner courtyards dripping with brilliant bougainvillea. There were numerous jewelry, crafts, and clothes shops, clearly catering to tourists and expatriates. You saw them in their shorts and T-shirts, their straw hats and sunglasses, in husband-and-wife couples, alone or in small groups, tan and well-fed, taking up the sidewalks as they passed.

The central square, the zocalo, however, was predominantly Mexican. It had newspaper vendors and people with small carts selling fresh fruit and nuts and candy. On the benches sat men reading papers or in conversation. The arcades on three sides of the square were packed with more vendors, selling the tackier forms of tourist souvenirs, sombreros, T-shirts, and tin jewelry. On the fourth side of the square was a church with a pinkish baroque facade.

I picked up a copy of Mexico City's newspaper, *La Jornada,* as well as the small English language weekly produced in San Andreas and chose a cafe down a side street from the zocalo to have a coffee. Unlike some of the other restaurants I'd seen while strolling around, this one didn't have big signs in Gringlish advertising margaritas and super-big enchiladas. The few tables were arranged around a fountain in a small courtyard. There were plenty of plants, a parrot, a simple menu.

After I'd read *La Jornada,* I turned to the San Andreas paper. It had a chatty local tone, much like any small town newspaper. The comings and goings of prominent San Andreans were noted, including the departure of Eleanor for Houston. There were a couple of art reviews of recent shows, a discussion of some traffic problems in a certain part of town, and mentions of many upcoming events. Eleanor had been right: there was a lot going on here, from yoga classes, to dance workshops, to readings. San Andreas was one of the Mexican towns where people came to learn Spanish. It had at least half a dozen language schools. Over the years a large expatriate community of mostly Americans, but also some Europeans, had built up. Some were older people who'd retired where their social security and pension dollars went a lot further, but many were artists and writers or would-be artists and writers.

I'm an expatriate myself, but I had never lived any place where sizable numbers of expats of the same nationality gathered together. It had always seemed to me that that would defeat the point, which is to leave your country behind.

I was just about to get up and leave when I noticed my name in the paper. For just a second I thought that it was another comings and goings tid-bit, as in Eleanor leaves and Cassandra and Lucy sublet her place. But then I saw that it was embedded in a small piece about a mystery writer, Colin Michaels, who was giving a reading tonight at the local arts center, El Centro Artistico.

"Long-time San Andreas resident Colin Michaels will read from his new mystery, *The Cassandra Caper.* Featuring his intrepid private investigator, Paul Roger, this new book opens with the dead body of a woman, Cassandra Reilly, washed up on a beach in Baja California. Cassandra was a go-go dancer in the seventies who has fallen on hard times, and it's up to Paul Roger to find the murderer in this exciting new thriller. Colin Michaels has written ten previous novels with Paul Roger."

"Lucy!" I said, when I got back to the house. "Somebody's trying to kill me!"

"What!" She had gotten up from her nap but hadn't progressed farther than a prone position on the sofa. It was as if the muscles and tendons that had been holding her upright had suddenly collapsed, all at once. She was reading an Agatha Christie mystery, in Spanish.

I handed her the local paper, and she read the short notice and began to laugh.

"A go-go dancer, hmm? Of course it's just a coincidence. Reilly's a common name."

"But Cassandra's not! Why do you think I chose it? No, the man must have somehow picked it up from one of the books I've translated. Those Gloria de los Angeles novels are everywhere."

"Well, you can't do anything now," Lucy said. "His novel's been published."

"I'll sue! I'll figure something out. I'll go to his reading and heckle him at least."

It was a useful ruse, anyway, to get Lucy out of the house.

◆

We ate dinner before the reading at a small restaurant I'd noticed near Eleanor's house. We had salads and enchiladas verdes and Tecate beer. Lucy said she could get more authentic food in San Francisco's Mission District, but she ate it. It gave her small comfort to speak Spanish with the waiter.

"I really don't feel I should be here," she said. "It was more wrenching than I imagined to leave the camp. I'd gotten so attached to the people. Cassandra, some of them have been living there for almost ten years, and they have no

idea when they'll be able to get back to their villages in
Guatemala. The conditions they're living in are tolerable, but
that's about all. Just by living in the camps, they're losing
their culture."

"You did what you could," I said. Small consolation.

"But I feel so guilty at having left! In three months I did
so little. If I didn't have my job in Oakland to get back to, I
would have stayed."

Two straight couples came into the restaurant and sat
down at the next table. They were middle-aged Americans.
Georgia's long letter to Lucy had said, "You'll love how easy
it is to meet people in San Andreas—everybody talks to
everybody!"

Apparently this was true, for our neighbors had no
problems breaking into our conversation, introducing
themselves, and telling us more than we ever wanted to
know about them. The Nelsons, long-time residents of San
Andreas, knew Eleanor well. "Oh yes, she's been a real force
in San Andreas." They glanced at each other briefly, and
Mrs. Nelson added brightly, "Without her and Colin, El
Centro Artistico never would have gotten off the ground the
way it has. People come from everywhere to take classes
there."

"We've only been here five years, but we just think it's
the best place on earth!" she went on. "Imagine—we've got
a maid and a gardener—we'd never be able to afford help in
the States, but here we hardly have to pay anything. Bob's
got his golf and I'm a volunteer at the library. One of the
things we love about San Andreas is that we hardly have to
know any Spanish. We're trying to persuade Lois and
George to move here. Even with the cost of living going up
here, they'll still be able to live so much better than at home."

"I love it," said Lois Palmer. "I've been taking a
ceramics class at the arts center, and a cooking class. I love
Mexican food, don't you? But George isn't so sure."

"Got a problem with the old ticker," said George. "I
know there are a couple of clinics, and one is for people like
us, but I'm still not convinced. What if I had a heart attack
on the street downtown and ended up at the Mexican
clinic?"

Lucy was too disgusted to even bother replying. And even if she had, she'd have been met by shocked surprise. "But we love Mexico and the Mexicans," they would say, puzzled. "They're such warm people, and their culture is so fascinating."

I jumped up with the check. "Well, we're off to a reading tonight," I said.

"That's right," said Mrs. Nelson, "Colin's reading. Well, you're in for a treat!"

♦

El Centro Artistico was a small but beautiful colonial-style structure, built around a courtyard landscaped with trees and plants. We went up a marble staircase to the second floor, where the reading was being held. It surprised me how many people were packed in the little room—a good seventy-five. Almost all of them were white, and many looked retirement age, but there were also a number of younger and middle-aged people. Many of them seemed to know each other and were deep in conversations, of which we caught snatches:

"First chapter is really coming along. Couple of good paragraphs today."

"Did you see what the Wallaces have done to their house? That incredible ceramic work. And they hardly had any trouble with the workmen."

Several people came up to us to chat, intrigued no doubt by the fact that Lucy was Latina ("We want the local people to always feel welcome at our events!"). For the first time in many years I felt peculiar about introducing myself and resorted to my given name, Catherine Frances.

"Are you an artist?" a woman with thick glasses and a rayon blouse printed with—yes, suitcases—asked me.

"Not even an amateur," I replied.

"Are you here to study Spanish?"

"No," I said reluctantly. No use telling her I made my living as a translator of Spanish literature; that could only lead to a discussion of the books I'd worked on and the revelation of my name. And I couldn't bear the news to spread so soon around the room, that I had become a fictional character.

♦

"Cassandra—or what had been Cassandra—was a worn-out bundle of varicose veins, needle tracks, and bunions. Her mottled face hung slackly, and even under the water you could see that she had a bad dye job."

Colin Michaels had been reading for about fifteen minutes when I decided to murder him. A short, red-faced man in his sixties, with a silky pompadour of white hair, he wore a short-sleeved Mexican shirt open in a V that showed his tan chest and white chest hair.

His character, Paul Roger, was different. Lanky, tough, laconic. You couldn't call Colin Michaels laconic by any stretch of the imagination. In fact, I began to think he was never going to shut up.

Finally he finished reading and it was time for questions. In order, he got: "Do you use a computer?" "How old were you when you started writing?" "How do you get an agent?" and "Have any of your books been made into films?" Then came one of those long-winded questions that isn't really a question but more a statement—if only you could figure out about what—on the part of the questioner.

Eventually it was my turn.

"I'm curious about where you came up with the name Cassandra Reilly for your victim."

"It's a great name, isn't it?" he said happily. "I have an Irish background myself so Reilly was obvious, but I think the choice of *Cassandra* was really quite inspired. Cassandra was the daughter of the King of Troy, who had the gift of prophecy, but not of being believed."

"I *know* who the mythical Cassandra was, thank you," I interrupted. "But did you realize that Cassandra Reilly is the real name of someone—someone I know quite well actually—yes, a very esteemed translator, the translator of Gloria de los Angeles magic realism novels. I'm sure the *real* Cassandra Reilly will be horribly upset when she hears that her name has been *stolen* and appended to the name of some dead go-go dancer!"

I sat down with a thump.

"Well, if I'm any judge of character," said Colin Michaels with a genial wink, "your friend will be flattered, not offended, to have her name appear in print."

A wave of mild laughter, meant to support Colin and dismiss me, flowed through the room, and he went on to the next question.

"I'm writing a mystery," a man said. "And I know I need to know about guns. I've read up on them, but I feel like I need to actually see one, to hold one, to fire one. . . ."

"To murder someone . . ." a voice added and everyone laughed.

"Do you have a gun?" the voice persevered. "Have you used one?"

Colin gave his genial smile. "Haven't you heard?" he said, "We mystery writers are the least violent people around. We keep it all in our heads!"

♦

Sometime after midnight that night there was a loud banging on the outside gate. Lucy was up and ready for bad news before I'd gotten my bathrobe on. When I finally managed to get downstairs, I saw her leading two uniformed policemen into the house.

"They found Eleanor off the highway to Mexico City," said Lucy in a flat tone. "In a motel room."

"What do you mean, they found her?" I stumbled and sat down on a woven footstool. "You mean, she wasn't really going to Houston at all? She was having a tryst?"

"When they found her she was dead," said Lucy, still trying to take it in. "Someone shot her through the heart."

♦

The police grilled us for an hour or two, not because they believed we were particularly guilty of anything, but because we might be able to give them information about Eleanor that would explain her death.

According to the police, the motel was a cheesy but not completely down and out place, on the outskirts of Mexico

City, near the airport, about four hours away from San Andreas. Had Eleanor just gone there to rest before her flight? It seemed likely, because she'd asked the receptionist to give her a wake-up call at ten p.m. When she didn't answer after several attempts, he knocked on the door, and finally, worried, let himself in. She'd been dead for several hours then. Had it been a random murder? A robbery as well? The police were inclined to think so. Her bags had been rifled through; so had the glove compartment of her car. It looked as if some jewelry might be missing. The Mexico City police were questioning all the motel's employees.

We couldn't help the police other than to let them look around Eleanor's house and take her address book. One of them, Officer Delgado, called her son's house in Houston. He began by speaking English but switched to Spanish in a minute.

When he put down the phone he said that her relatives would be flying in tomorrow.

"He spoke Spanish to you," I commented.

"No, her son was away on business," said Delgado. "That was his wife."

♦

At seven the next morning Eleanor's housekeeper Rosario let herself in. She hadn't heard the news yet, and had to sit down at first when we told her. "What a terrible death," she said, making the sign of the cross. Rosario was about Eleanor's age, perhaps a little younger. She had smooth black hair in a bun and a sturdy, slow-moving body. We thought she would want to go home, but instead, after a glass of water, she rose and began the work of dusting and straightening, all the while murmuring, "How terrible."

We watched for a moment, unsure whether she was mourning Eleanor the person or just reacting to the horror of the situation. "I'm not sure you need to do anything now," Lucy told her gently.

"But people will be coming," Rosario said. "Her son will finally come back now, and Isabella."

"Isabella?" I asked. "Is that his wife?"

"Yes," said Rosario, "She comes from San Andreas."

♦

Eleanor's death sent a chill of fear through the expatriate community. In whispered conversations in the expensive restaurants and shops, they told each other that they weren't surprised. The flip side of their belief that the Mexicans were warm and happy people was their conviction that the whole country seethed with thieves and murderers. That afternoon Colin Michaels called a community meeting at El Centro Artistico, and the room was packed.

"We've got to pressure the police to solve this murder quickly," he said. "The mayor of San Andreas is at the coast at the moment, but his assistant agrees—the death of one American is a horrible blow to the image of Mexican tourism."

Colin's face was flushed a strawberry color, and his voice was shrill. "A member of our peaceful little community has been murdered," he said. "We could be next!"

I bumped into him on purpose after the meeting. "Oh, the friend of Cassandra Reilly's," he said. "I'm sorry, I didn't catch your name. You and your friend have been staying at Eleanor's. How very upsetting for you."

"You knew her well, it sounds like," I said.

"Oh everyone knew Eleanor," he said. "She was a fixture. An absolute fixture. We discovered San Andreas years ago, both of us; we were the early ones. We had a chance to really mold it to become the place it is now. Without Eleanor, this arts center wouldn't exist. I can't believe, I just can't believe, she's gone."

"Then you know about her son and his wife," I said. "What was that story again?"

"I always liked the girl myself," said Colin. "It was her mother, her whole family, that was the problem. Greedy, always taking advantage of whatever kindness Eleanor showed them. The girl herself . . ."

"Isabella?"

"Yes. She was so young. It was her mother who had ambitions, who made sure to leave the two young people together so that the inevitable happened."

"Isabella's mother is local then?"

"Why yes. You must have met her. Rosario, the woman who cleans—cleaned—for Eleanor."

I remembered Rosario's stunned face but deep-down lack of feeling about Eleanor's death, how her dark eyes had looked past us to something on a table or a shelf, something terribly familiar, that was now missing. "Where are the figures?" she had asked. "Señora Harrington's sculptures?"

"I put them away yesterday," Lucy had admitted. "I didn't . . . like to look at them."

"Ah," Rosario had said. "*Bueno.*"

♦

When I got back to the house I found Lucy talking with the gardener. "This is Isabella's brother, Juan," she said. "He has a degree in English literature, but hasn't been able to find work."

Juan wore a Grateful Dead T-shirt and an earring in one ear. "My sister is always trying to get me to come to the States to live. I don't mind visiting, but I wouldn't want to live there. I'd rather live in my own country. Not that San Andreas always feels like Mexico."

"Did the whole family work for Eleanor?" I asked Lucy when Juan had left for the day. "And if Rosario and Juan were her relatives as well as her employees, why would Eleanor feel she needed people to housesit for her?"

"I don't know whether it was a question of trust, or of trying to make a few extra dollars. Do you remember how quick she snatched up our check yesterday?"

"But she has tons of money! Doesn't she? She must just employ them as a favor to her son."

Her son. Something that had been nagging at me all day rose to the surface. "And where was he in the middle of the night anyway? Away on business. Does anyone know where?"

♦

Isabella and her two young daughters arrived that night after dinner and came straight to the house. Lucy and I were ready to leave, but she insisted we stay.

"No, you must stay, please," she said. "Allen would want it."

"But at a time like this—we'd only be in the way."

"At least until tomorrow," she said urgently.

I wondered if she were afraid to stay in the house by herself.

Isabella was an attractive woman of about thirty, dressed for travel in a simple dress and sandals. Her black hair was fashionably cut, and she had a warm but slightly imposing air. I couldn't imagine her putting up with any shit from Eleanor.

After she got her two girls off to bed, she came back downstairs, now wearing jeans, her eyes taking in the room as she descended.

"It hasn't changed," she said. "In ten years, it hasn't really changed. Still the beautiful home I admired in my silly way when I used to come here with my mother to help her clean it. Everything so tasteful, so beautiful. So artistic, I thought. The home of an artist." She laughed shortly. "But what happened to her sculptures, all those Indian women in serapes with their baskets full of tortillas?"

"I put them away," said Lucy.

Isabella sat down, but her tiredness didn't cause her to slump. "I'm embarrassed to tell you that I really liked them, that summer I was twenty. I didn't have much consciousness about anything. Allen was just about as innocent as I was. 'Oh, my mother will adore you,' he kept telling me.

"My own mother told me different, but I didn't pay any attention to her. She was right, of course, not Allen. When Eleanor came back from her vacation and found out what had been going on for two months, she threw me out. She couldn't believe that Allen followed. She never believed it. Even when she came for her annual visit to Houston, she tried not to see me or the kids if she could avoid it."

"Where is Allen, by the way?" I put in, as casually as I could.

Isabella's eyes shifted slightly, but her tone seemed straightforward. "He was a little hard to track down. As a matter of fact, he's right here in Mexico. In Cancun. He's driving up to San Andreas tonight." She took a long breath, which made me realize she'd been holding it. "The company he works for, a hotel chain, is always sending him on the road."

♦

"You realize, he's the one who did it," I told Lucy that night when we were alone. "He must have hated his mother for what she did to his wife."

"It takes a lot more than hatred to kill someone," said Lucy, from the twin bed next to me. "Sure he 'disappointed' her by marrying a Mexican, but why would he kill his mother over it ten years later? If he really did kill her, it was for some other reason. Money, for instance. How well-off was Eleanor really, and what about Allen himself? Is he in debt? Does he have a drug habit? Would inheriting Eleanor's money help him?" Lucy held up the Agatha Christie she was reading. "I used to read lots of these in medical school. They probably gave me a distorted view of crime—that it was all about entailed estates and hidden relatives—but at bottom they said something true—people are more likely to kill for money than for passion."

♦

Allen Harrington had still not arrived by the time I woke up in the morning and headed out for my morning coffee. Lucy got up at the same time and went off to to the local clinic. "I'll just have them check me out," she said. "And then, maybe, I'll see if they need me to volunteer at all while we're here."

"You just can't keep away from work," I teased her, but I was still worried. What if there was something really wrong with her?

As luck would have it, I discovered Colin Michaels in the cafe I'd gone to yesterday. He was drinking a large Bloody Mary and eating eggs and bacon. No wonder every capillary on his face was broken.

"Hello, friend of Cassandra Reilly," he greeted me. "We've got to stop meeting like this."

"Tell me about Eleanor's son," I said, sitting down next to him and ordering *café con leche*. "You said you'd known her since the early days here. You must have known her son when he was growing up."

"Oh, he didn't grow up here," said Colin, a little too quickly. "I mean, he came in the summers. But otherwise, he went to a boarding school in the States. Eleanor didn't want him to go to school in San Andreas. She wanted him to have a proper education."

"If Eleanor was around fifty and her son is around thirty," I said, thinking aloud, "She must have been fairly young when she had him."

"I suppose so," said Colin, bending over his food.

"What about Mr. Harrington?" I said suddenly. "Nobody says anything about a Mr. Harrington. I always assumed that Eleanor had gotten her money from her husband, that she was a wealthy widow."

"Believe the money came from her family," said Colin. "Parents set her up here, wanted her out of Houston, I suppose. But myself, I've always believed that the past is past. We all have our reasons to have settled in San Andreas. Now, myself . . ."

"Oh, I see," I said slowly. "Yes, of course. There was no Mr. Harrington. Eleanor's son Allen was born out of wedlock."

"What's past is past," said Colin and ordered another drink. It was only nine in the morning.

You could be a drunk anywhere, but it must be more pleasant, and cheaper, in San Andreas.

◆

Allen Harrington drove up at noon. Did I have a reason for assuming he'd be white? Only my own ethnocentrism. He was a compact, dark-skinned man, darker than his wife, with startling green eyes.

"What a nightmare," he said, as he paced around the room. "What a way for my mother to die. Have they found out anything more about the man who killed her? I'm going down to the police station in a few minutes. I'll make them take this seriously."

Don't overdo it, Allen, I thought.

Isabella tried to soothe him. "I'm sure the police are doing all they can."

"But what kind of a country is this, that people can't check into a motel room without being robbed and murdered?"

"The police seem to think she knew her attacker," I said, and Lucy stared at me to hear such a bold-faced lie.

"They do?" Allen shouted at his wife. "You didn't tell me this. Who killed my mother? Juan? Your worthless cousin Pedro?"

For answer, Isabella turned on her heel and marched out of the house.

"That was a harsh thing to say," said Lucy.

Allen stared at us a moment and then, unable to defend himself, burst into agitated tears.

When he calmed down, he said, "I loved my mother. I know she wasn't a particularly good person. In some ways, I admit, she wrecked my life. But she was still my mother."

"Who was your father, Allen?" I asked.

"I don't know. My mother may not have known herself. She came down to Mexico when she was nineteen or twenty for a few weeks of partying, and ended up getting pregnant. By the time she realized it, she was too far along for an abortion. The Harringtons are a prominent family in Houston. The agreement was that if she stayed in Mexico, they'd set up a trust fund for her, and she agreed. It was a crazy mix of shame and pride that kept her here. She loved Mexico and she hated it. The only way she could stay here was to stay separate and to bond with the other white expatriates. She never felt quite accepted here though—that's why she sent me away to school."

Allen looked at his arm, which was the color of walnut. "She couldn't ever really see me, see who I was. When I wanted to marry Isabella, she said, 'You can't marry a Mexican.'

"'Mother,' I said. 'I *am* a Mexican.'

"'No you're not,' she said. 'You're white. You don't even speak Spanish. You have dual citizenship. You belong in America.'

"I didn't speak much Spanish then. Meeting Isabella changed me. I learned Spanish and found a job that would let me travel in Mexico."

"Isabella said you were in Cancun."

He looked at me oddly, and almost aggressively, with those brilliant green eyes. "You need proof? You think *I* was somehow involved in this?"

"Don't be ridiculous," broke in Lucy calmly. "Cassandra was just asking a question."

"I'm sorry," he said, calming down. "I apologize. And now, if you'll excuse me," he said. "I also need to apologize to my wife."

♦

Dr. Rodriguez, Antonia Rodriguez, the head doctor at the local clinic, had said Lucy seemed to be suffering from exhaustion and a slight case of anemia, nothing more. But she had sent a blood sample to Mexico City anyway. Meanwhile, she didn't exactly say no to Lucy helping her out a couple of hours every morning. The clinic was seriously underfunded, unlike the private clinic that the expatriates all went to.

"It makes me feel better to do something," Lucy said. "Otherwise I'd go crazy here."

But even working two hours was tiring to her, and when she came back to the small hotel where we'd moved after Allen arrived, she usually lay on the bed reading Agatha Christie.

I kept waiting for the police to announce that Allen Harrington had killed his mother. Who else would have know she was stopping at that motel? Who else would have persuaded Eleanor to open her door to him?

But the days passed and no murder suspect was named.

The next issue of the local English paper came out with an angry editorial by Colin Michaels and with letters to the editor that bemoaned the days when San Andreas had been a safe little town. "I left Los Angeles because of the crime . . . and what do I find here?"

There was a small notice near the back of the paper that made me pause. It said that the bulk of Mrs. Harrington's estate would go toward expanding the arts center. An auditorium for readings would be added, and a new library specializing in English books. Colin Michaels, president of the board of El Centro Artistico, expressed his pleasure and said that, in honor of Eleanor's bequest, the new center would be named after Mrs. Harrington.

I decided to visit the little newspaper office and asked for the managing editor.

"I don't know what their relationship was," she admitted. "I've only been here a few years, and Colin and Eleanor went back thirty years. You might talk to one of the past editors. Dora James started the paper in the early seventies. She remembers everything."

♦

"Oh, they had quite the feud going once," Dora James said. "Eleanor had the money, but Colin had the name. He was one of the biggest names to settle in San Andreas. Not that he was so incredibly successful anyplace but here. But that's one reason people settle here, you know. In the States Colin was just another mystery writer; here he was famous. They both wanted to control the arts center. This year Colin was president, but last year she was. It was essentially harmless, their bickering and wrangling. Though I must admit, I'd heard that the victim in Colin's latest novel, *The Cassandra Caper*, was an unflattering portrait of Eleanor. He must feel terrible now. Especially since she left the arts center all that money."

Well, at least I knew now that Eleanor really had been rich. But where did her giving most of her money to the arts center leave Allen?

Dora James shook her head. "Have you ever read any of Colin's mysteries? They really don't improve. I always end up feeling as if I've missed something crucial in understanding the plot. But it's usually because Colin has forgotten it himself. What he needs, you know," she smiled, "is a good editor."

◆

I found Allen with Isabella in the house, where they were packing up Eleanor's things. "Yes, I know about the bequest," he said. "The house is mine though. We're giving it to Rosario."

I asked him if his mother ever talked much about Colin Michaels.

"Oh, old Colin," said Allen. "They were lovers all during my childhood. They had a terrible fight sometime during the seventies. They'd helped create the arts center together, you see. But they couldn't agree how to run it. The last I heard, Mother was going to pull all her money out of it. She told me she'd been talking to a lawyer in Mexico City. I didn't believe that she really would. It was just something she used against Colin. Her feud with him had been going on for years. But the arts center really meant something to her. And judging from her will, she really did want almost everything to go into expanding it."

I didn't know how to ask for the name of the lawyer, but he gave it to me anyway as he went on, "One of the maids says she saw a man with a black mustache and dark hat slipping down the corridor sometime late in the afternoon that day. I thought maybe it could have been my mother's lawyer, Jorge Salinas, because he has a big black mustache, but his secretary confirmed he'd been in his office all day. It was probably just something the maid made up to make herself sound more interesting."

◆

When I called Jorge Salinas, he admitted that Mrs. Harrington had talked to him recently, but he wouldn't say about what. They had had no appointment that day, he said. His records could confirm it.

"Just tell me this," I asked. "Would you have been surprised if Mrs. Harrington had stopped into your office that day?"

"No," he said finally. "I guess I would not have been surprised."

♦

It was time to go to the police. Delgado was skeptical. "Señor Michaels has an alibi for the time Mrs. Harrington was murdered. He was here in San Andreas, reading to a large crowd, in a program that had been arranged for weeks."

"Mrs. Harrington left San Andreas at ten in the morning. At a little before two she checked into the motel. You think she died around six. But what if she died earlier, at three? That would have given him four hours to get back to San Andreas."

"It's a possibility," Delgado allowed. "But there are no witnesses."

"Get a search warrant," I said. "It can't do any harm. If Colin is the mystery writer Dora James says he is, he will have made a mistake in his plotting and forgotten some crucial little element. He's no Agatha Christie."

♦

At first I thought I'd made a bad mistake. The police searched Colin's house and car for four hours and found nothing incriminating. No weapon. None of Eleanor's jewelry. No tell-tale copy of a will that she was carrying to her lawyer's. It was only by chance that one of the cops happened to open the freezer. There, back in the corner, was a false black mustache, that for reasons of vanity or foolishness, Colin had not been able to bring himself to throw away.

♦

The maid identified him and even though he never confessed, insisting that the mustache was a joke left over from Halloween, Colin soon found himself in the courtroom and then in prison, a place he'd always described from the outside. The Harrington Arts Center expanded without him, though apparently he continues to write murder mysteries from prison while appealing his life sentence.

I heard all this from Lucy, who made a fast friend of the Dr. Antonia Rodriguez, the doctor at the San Andreas clinic. Lucy visits her regularly, on her way to and from the refugee camp on the Guatemala border, where she now spends three months every year.

An Evening Out

Victoria A. Brownworth

Dusk had pressed itself into dark an hour before.
Fingering the density of the autumn night was the smolder of
burning leaves.

Jane Etting felt the acridity as if it were a scrim hanging
in the air above her bare shoulders.

She sat at the vanity, holding a bottle of perfume.
Something small and floral and costly. The flat black stares
of the uncurtained windows flanked the triptych of her
image in the mirror. One window stood half-open in a dead
wink. No discernible sounds entered through it, just a steady
whooshing of traffic and the scent of smoke.

It was just past six on a Friday night in mid-October in a
sprawling fourteenth-floor apartment off Central Park in
New York. From where she sat, gripping the perfume bottle,
dressed in a strapless black bra and an ankle-length black
half-slip, Jane could see nothing but herself and the empty
eyes of the windows behind her.

If she had stood and walked to the windows, if she
looked out briefly before pulling together the chilled damask
of the ash-of-roses drapes, she would see the dark velvet void
of the park, the pavé crust of city lights, the sleek and silken
lines of traffic. As she closed the drapes she would pull back
just enough to see the disembodied Jane against the
windows: one white arm raised, an angle of neck and

shoulder, a blurred wing of hair—then nothing, as cloth met cloth in a dusty kiss.

But she did not stand, did not stir from the torpor of the vanity seat where she had held the perfume bottle so long its scent had heated from her grip.

Tony was late. Ten minutes had ambled toward twenty and now slipped languorously forward to the half hour. Dinner was at eight; cocktails began at seven.

He should be here, she thought, finally lifting the lid from her scent, spraying a fog-fine mist over her neck and shoulders. It was the the only action she felt able to take.

He should pull those damned drapes closed, she thought. He should bring me Lillet with ice and a twist *and he should not be late.*

The thoughts came in a rush, like the traffic sounds behind and below her. They registered, but without clarity, without definition. She was not angry.

Dinner was at eight and Jane wanted a cocktail now, instead of the too-sweet taste of Norell in her mouth. She touched her fingers to her cheekbones, lightly, tentatively, as if probing for a flaw, a small scar, a break in the white-on-white porcelain pattern of her face. But she felt nothing beyond the slight razor pressure of her lacquered fingernails and the velvet pads of her cheeks. She put her palms flat on the cool mahogany of the table, staring at the three faces of Jane in the angled mirror. She took in Jane's short russet hair exposing her white throat, examined the slate-gray eyes, the long slender nose, the mouth full-lipped, yet elegant.

This was what Tony saw, she thought as she set emerald studs into each ear. This is what Tony had seen from a fifth-row center seat at the ballet thirteen years ago. This is what Tony had married eleven years earlier. This was who Tony was taking to Colin and Diana's for a sit-down dinner for twenty patrons of the Museum Archives. This was who Tony would bed sometime after one between the chill sheets on the queen-sized bed made from Brentwood ash in their bedroom. This.

She stared at herself, at the black and red and white that stood so stark against the uncurtained windows.

♦

When Tony walked through the door with a drink in
each hand at 6:40, he saw the slender white back of his wife,
the line of vertebrae a slight shadow above and below the
thin black line of her bra. He saw the vee and arc of her
upswept wing of hair and the quick glint of an earring as her
head moved almost imperceptibly when he entered the
room. It was the same swan-like look he had first registered
as she spun *jetés* across the stage in London.

It was far more than lust that swept him as he saw her.
He felt it keenly, like possession, knew he wanted to possess
her in turn.

My darling, he thought, as he sat a Lillet with a twist
next to her right hand and brushed against her shoulder ever
so lightly with his hip as he bent down.

"Sorry I'm late, love," he said instead as he walked
toward the drapes and the open window. "Emlen called as I
was leaving the office and I needed to sort that out before I
left. Traffic's a crawl and the taxi took absolutely *days*."

◆

Jane registered, as she always did, the Britishisms that
remained after twenty years in New York, registered the
inflection, rather than the accent itself, registered the place
on her upper arm where she had felt the wool of his trousers
against her skin. Jane registered a chill.

"I won't say you might have called, but you might
have," she said, still staring at herself and the three oblongs
of dusty rose behind her. She sipped her drink, the smell of
oranges almost too fresh and raw. She felt her throat tighten.

"In thirteen years of knowing you I have yet to know
you to call," she said, orange zest tingling on the edge of her
tongue, her color just a touch darker as she drank a little
more. "I thought you Brits were so punctual. Or is this what
is meant by 'sixish'," she said, her voice devoid of inflection.

◆

Tony stood a half room away, buttoning up his evening
shirt as he turned toward the edge in her voice. He smelled
oranges, gardenia, and yes, burning leaves. He ran his right

hand up to his temple but did not touch his dark hair, his arm stopping in mid-movement, as if the register of his own inchoate surprise.

Jane continued to sit with her back toward her husband, although she could see his every movement in the mirror. Her glass was nearly empty.

"Some people *divorce* over rudeness, you know," she said, the words only slightly less foreign to her than they were to him.

She knew then, as she saw him start toward her, tall, his hair still fully black at forty-eight, his shirt only half-buttoned, that he was going to make love to her. She saw in his walk, in the slight tightness of it, that he wanted her, that he was thinking of an excuse for Diana, that he had not, in fact, heard what she had said, or if he had, had not heard *how* she had said it. A small breath of orange passed over her lips.

♦

Tony was struck by the urgency of his own feelings. *Divorce.* The word had riven him. No—the casual way she had said it. Humorless. Without anger either. She *meant* it, he knew.

He was alarmed. He had to touch her suddenly, as if putting flesh to flesh were more implacable than any arrangement of sounds that came from her.

He stopped just short of her chair and said, "It *is* my fault but we're going to be late, darling, so *do* get dressed." He caught a subtle breath of orange. He thought it might strangle him.

♦

Jane was relieved when she realized Tony was not going to touch her, but her sigh was inaudible.

"I'll get my dress then," she said, standing for the first time in over an hour, her thighs and buttocks numb from strain. She moved simply, her legs and arms and torso fluid, unlike other dancers who were often so awkward when they moved offstage. She did not turn her head in his direction.

She could feel the heat of him from where she stood at the closet door.

♦

Could it happen like this, he thought. Could he just come in from the office of an evening a few minutes late and find his marriage was over, the woman he loved changed? Yet even as he asked himself the question, he knew that everything *was* changed. Between the time Emlen called him about the Cavendar proposal to the point at which the taxi had passed round Columbus Circle, he had lost her. He had handed her the drink that had given her the courage to end it.

It could not be.

"You'll want another drink before we leave, I'll wager," he said as he picked up her glass, the thick twist of orange angled in the glass, somehow hideous under the mark of her lips, like a scrap of flesh or a scar disembodied from its wound. He nearly dropped the glass.

♦

"Yes, I would," Jane answered him, sure now that if she kept her back to him she could recover herself enough—that they could dress and leave and spend the evening wooing the patrons with Colin and Diana over salmon and champagne and whatever else the *haute monde* were eating these days. If she kept herself free of him she would recover, she thought, as she slipped her evening dress over her head. But she was still unsure what those words meant: recover, free, divorce. She had been unsure what would happen when she had walked from the stage thirteen years ago in London. For ten years she had danced only this ballet, this same *pas de deux*. She stood before the cheval mirror now, a woman of thirty-seven. She was not at the *barre*, she was not on the stage, she was not sure which *jeté* would be her exit.

Tony poured Jane another Lillet and made himself a very dry double martini. Gin always helped clear his head in a way scotch never did. He looked round their living room as he sipped the gin and refilled his glass, as if he were looking for an escape. He needed time to sort this out. But there was no time. He looked at his Rolex. Just seven. If they were to get to dinner at Diana's across the Park, they had to leave by the half-hour, twenty-till at the latest.

Tony looked at the room they had spent so many evenings in, alone and with friends. It *was* a room they had lived-in, and now he searched it as if it were the only map that could show him how to get where he needed to go—searched for a way out, a way back to his wife, searched for a place to plug the fault that threatened to sunder his life.

Tony took the drinks back to the dressing room. If the first drink had begun the first fissure, perhaps the second could cement it.

Jane was there in the doorway between the dressing room and the bath as he entered. A ring of soft lights circled the mirror that stretched the length of the double sinks. From where he stood he could see not only his wife's back, now dressed in a straight satin sheath of an evening gown of a rich forest green edged in black and gold at the bodice. He could also see, for the first time, his wife's face, reflected in the bathroom mirror.

From where he stood, he could see her face, see her staring at herself and past herself, but she could not see him. He was not reflected from where she stood.

It was like it had been the first time he had seen her, when six of them had gone to the ballet together and there she had been before him. He had seen her, watched her for all the hours of the ballet, but she had not seen him. Seeing him had made a difference.

He had gone backstage with the others and Diana had introduced them. She had stood much as she was now, her back to him, her neck arched, her then-long hair in a tight red twist. And when she had turned to take his hand he had felt the heat of her response and he had known he could win her.

Now he moved into her periphery, walked to her, handed her the drink, careful not to touch her as he did so. The air around her felt cool, but it was warm near the theatrical lights of the bath.

♦

Jane felt him behind her before she actually saw him in the mirror. *Turn toward him*, she commanded herself. Turn and go. Walk past him, don't touch him, don't let him touch you. Simply go.

It was what Jane had told herself the first night she had met him, when her friend from the Academy had brought him backstage. Diana had led him in with Colin and some other friends. She had seen him in the mirror and had been struck by how handsome he was, struck by his strength and by a desire to capture that. "Virile," Diana had said to her *soto voce* in the dressing room. "Don't take it seriously."

But when Jane had turned and taken Tony's hand there had been something in it, some small tremor that had alerted her to his desire and she had told herself to let it go, to leave, to not even begin with a drink or a chat in a too-loud pub in Covent Garden.

Go, she had commanded herself, you are a dancer, this is the interval, not the main piece. And then she was married, back in New York, and off the stage for good.

She looked into the lights, into the mirror. Her eyes met Tony's in the glass. The air from the open window wound its way through the drapes and snaked up her back. In her right hand the drink shook with a delicate *frisson*, orange peel slithering in the amber liquid.

"I'll just have this drink then and do my face and we'll be off, alright," she said to the figure retreating from the mirror.

She moved into the bath, setting her drink to the right of the first sink, her hands shaking then lifting it almost immediately to drink.

The bottle green of her dress heightened the whiteness of her skin. She stood, slender and still, looking into the glass as if it were a gypsy crystal, as if it were the exit Alice had sought, as if it could take away the fortune she had read in her husband's face a moment before.

She took another drink, lifted a fat sable brush from a jar under the lights and ran it over a cake of pale russet blush. She dusted each cheekbone, touched her temples lightly by her hair. She outlined her lips with a brick-colored pencil, then filled them in with a subtly lighter shade, deftly blending the lines with her fingertip.

Her eyes were done, darkening with drink, with the reflection of her dress, with whatever it was she had read in Tony's eyes. The Jane that returned her gaze was the Jane of hundreds of skilled performances, the Jane of daring leaps and silken splits, the Jane who spun onto stage with a fever of 103°, the Jane who danced for forty minutes on a torn tendon, the Jane who knew how to walk by admirers without stopping, who knew how to quench desire with a sigh or a kiss. This Jane turned fully round, drink in one hand, evening bag in the other, glanced at her watch—7:25—and walked in one easy movement to the center of the dressing room saying, "Time we moved on, isn't it, Tony?" and looked at her husband dead on.

♦

He had needed to walk away after she had looked at him over her drink in the doorway. He had seen her shudder, felt the wave of her revulsion hit him with the force of hurricane. He had felt an almost physical need to right himself, to steady his entire being against something solid—the doorframe, the French armoire, a chair, anything.

So he had retreated to the window, thrown back the drapes, and opened the window even further, full-sash. He had hung his head over the sill and breathed in the smell that reminded him of a lifetime of bonfire nights in London, the smell that took him back to an evening just before he had asked Jane to quit the ballet and marry him and go back to New York.

It was bonfire night and all of London was hung with the scrim of a thousand small fires in back gardens from Hackney to Kensington. Diana had coaxed Colin over from the States, and the four of them had gone to Alexandria Palace to watch the fireworks because it was where Diana had first seen them as a child.

He had held Jane in his arms that night on a small crest of hill and she had told him later that she had never felt fireworks before like that, had never been so close to them. "Not even on Independence Day?" he had asked her and she had averted her eyes and said, "You don't understand. These weren't the same. These were small. These were *not* spectacular. These I could have to myself." He had never really understood what she'd meant by that and he knew it flawed him somehow in her eyes.

Now as he smelled that smell of night and autumn he wanted it to do over again, wanted to just listen to her, not ask the questions that set them apart from each other, but just hold her in his arms as he had that night. She had loved him that night—he had felt it in the way she had pressed against him the way the dusk pressed into dark—something perfect and ordinary.

He wanted that now—he wanted to bring her here to the window, to hold her in front of him, his arms tight around her, the lights of the city beyond like the cascading embers of the fireworks and all around them the scent of that first bonfire night they had spent together, like the scent in a room after making love.

Tony turned from the window, straightening his dinner jacket and reaching for his glass on the wine table left of the drapes. As he did so he saw his wife step into the center of the dressing room and stop, staring directly at him, searching out his eyes, locking his gaze with hers.

Darling, he breathed to himself. I can stop this now, he thought, I know how to stop it all now. He moved forward, sure now that he could recapture her, sure that it could all happen before they even left for dinner. Sure he had the strength that had first drawn her to him.

◆

"Jane," she heard him call to her from the window, on which the drapes had been pulled back.

The window, which she always left open half-way no matter what the temperature, was flung wide, the October air fluttering the drapes of the other windows and ruffling Tony's hair.

The smell of burning leaves was stronger now and mingled with the smell of oranges in the air, heady and overpowering, making her suddenly dizzy. She was hungry, they were going to be late and Diana was going to be solidly angry if they didn't leave almost immediately. She had to get out, she had to keep moving forward.

"Tony," she said, her voice lower and softer than she had meant it to be. "Isn't it time we left?" This last was more straightforward, but he did not hear it, he was back at the window, saying her name again, drawing her to him.

♦

Peripherally he could see her almost glide forward as he heard her voice, low and sensual, say his name in response. She had caught the scent, too, he saw it, saw her step and sniff the air, like an animal does in the woods. He saw her response, visceral.

They were moving toward each other now, he could sense it, they were recovering whatever ground had fissured beneath them in the last hour, in the last decade. This was the moment of recovery, of seizure, of securing what they had had and lost. They would arrive at Diana and Colin's revivified, a couple in love. He could smell the change in the air, like rain before a storm.

Jane followed the scent as she walked toward the window and Tony. That smell is like London, she thought, like the Tube always threatening fire. Something in the scent made her uneasy. It was atavistic, she thought, the aversion to fire. Like sensing death.

"It's time we moved on," she said again, "to Diana's," her hand raised, almost touching his arm. Now his back was to her. She was suddenly nervous about what she would see when he turned around. Near the window the air had changed. It was too chill. The smoke so pungent.

It was slow, the way he moved in a simple arc of arm and shoulder. Slow too the way he grasped her firmly by her shoulders and swung her toward him. He was so strong.

She hadn't expected him to touch her. She dropped the empty glass, orange peel slithering across the parquet like something poisonous and feral. Her evening bag was cast in a silken line of gold and green into the mahogany wine table, overturning it.

♦

"Tony," she said, her voice almost inaudible, more like the whoosh of the traffic below than the urgent signal she pulsed forward.

This was enough, she knew. He should not have touched her. If he hadn't, she might have recovered, she might have gone on—to dinner, to bed, to the next anniversary. It had spun out of her control now, like the glass on the wood floor, like a *jeté* begun too fast. There was injury ahead if she didn't stop it now, she knew.

It could not be. "Tony," she said, her voice soft and firm, strong as his arms around her. "Tony, I'm leaving."

♦

He had her in his arms now, they were surrounded again by the chill of an autumn night, the heady fragrance of a city on fire, the shattered filaments of fireworks or stars or the lights of the town outside. All the elements were there, only this time he would not ask the question, this time he would only repeat what she had told him then.

"I have never felt it like this before," he breathed into her hair. She was shrouded by scent, a veil of oranges, gardenia, and something burning. He turned her around to face him, heard her saying his name, telling him they must be leaving.

"I love you," he said just before he kissed her, her mouth as cool as the night, the exotic taste of oranges and gardenias alive on her tongue. *I love you*, he thought, tasting her, recapturing her, seizing their lives with his kiss. Her arms were tight within his. He had them both now, he propelled them forward.

His lips released hers and she stood before him, as close as she could ever be, and he saw her face—the white and red like hot flame.

"Tony, we have to go," she said, her voice even, controlled. *Let me go*, she thought, let me go and I will walk away, I will not look back.

His lips descended to her hair, her neck as he pushed her against the thin frame of wood between the windows.

It was then that Jane shivered. Then that the cold air overtook her bare shoulders and neck, chilling her to the roots of her hair.

He felt it, the shudder, and released her suddenly, so that she was held against the window frame only by his body positioned before hers.

"Tony," she spoke quietly now, her voice as flat as she could make it. "You must call Diana," she went on. "You must tell her we won't be coming." He heard neither fear nor promise.

He looked at her full in the face then, taking in the eyes so deeply gray they looked black in the faint light from the bath. Her skin held a slight flush, but a wave of pink, rather than a mottling. Her lips were apart, the lipstick pressed from them by his kiss. Her hair was mussed and green and gold glinted from her right ear.

The question came before he could stop it. "You don't love me, then?" Only the inflection made it more than a statement as he looked at her, feeling his lips move, hearing the words fall between them like embers.

"You don't understand," she whispered, a bitter orange mist rising from between her lips.

It overpowered him then—he had been so sure he could set it right and there it was—the ghastly, strangling response, the very words she had said that night. And that smell—he wanted to bite it back, he was choking on it.

There was some inchoate mix of sounds from him as he pulled her back into his arms. They resonated in the muffling folds of the drapes as he grabbed at her. She said nothing—she neither said his name nor cried nor screamed as she fell through the window in a thirty-second spin into the street below.

Through the open window came the steady whooshing sound of traffic, like waves cresting and falling. Then the sharp staccato of a distant siren growing nearer.

♦

Tony stood for a time looking out onto the crumpled fabric of the night, glittering and dark. Then he turned, looked at his watch, and walked toward the telephone.

THE POOL

Ruthann Robson

It is never clean enough for her. There is always at least a splayed leaf floating until it becomes saturated and sinks to the bottom like a shadow without an object. Sometimes there is an insect, a dragonfly with its wet wings furiously beating as if its life depends on flight; or a yellow-jacket with its stripes fading into a pale blue. Once there was a frog, bloated with death. She ignored it until Tina came home, and after dinner, sitting on the concrete deck in the twilight drinking Kahlua and coffee, she casually pointed it out to Tina, as if she had just then noticed it. Tina, predictably and stoically, got the net and fished out the stiff amphibian. Tina deposited the animal in the tall grass that leaned against the wall that surrounded the pool which Tina never used. Tina, freckled white, did not even like to sunbathe near the pool's reflective glare. She burnt easily.

Augusta, Tina's lover, had beige flesh that tanned slowly but successfully. Augusta swam. Augusta spent her daylight summer hours studying the water in the pool or the absence of reflections on the gray wall. The wall did not seem tall enough to Augusta. It was the legal limit, according to Tina, but Augusta wondered what a therapist knew about the law. Augusta thought that perhaps they should break glass bottles, preferably thick liquor bottles, into sharp pieces and cement them to the top of the wall. Augusta had seen this in

Mexico, and even then she had thought it attractively useful. Tina disapproved of the idea. Augusta idly plotted its execution.

Even with the frog gone, the pool reminds Augusta of a fouled pond. She complains to Tina, who does not answer. Annoyed, Augusta retreats and pours the remains of her cold coffee and Kahlua into the kitchen sink. She goes to bed, without Tina. Augusta later listens to Tina's familiar voice modulate with the intimacy of conversation. Tina must be on the phone to her newest, Augusta thinks, almost without rancor, as she falls asleep.

In the morning, after Tina is gone, Augusta telephones the pool company.

It is still morning when Augusta and the pool woman find themselves—and each other—on the kitchen floor, a few steps from the tinted sliding glass doors that separate the house from the pool. The women roll dangerously close to the garbage container. Augusta can smell the salty ocean, which she first thinks is seeping from the pool woman, until she remembers the shrimp she shelled for Tina's dinner last night.

The image of Tina sucking the butter off her fingers after eating each shrimp brings no flashes of guilt to Augusta, even as Augusta licks the long thumb of the pool woman. Tina and Augusta are fervently nonmonogamous; guilt and jealousy have been exiled from their open marriage. Their only boundaries are the ethical ones born of their individual professions. Tina does not have sexual relations with her patients, at least not until the therapeutic relationship has been terminated for six months. Augusta does not have sexual relations with her students, at least not until the woman has graduated the college and there is no possibility the former student would be anything other than former.

Augusta's *modus operandi* is well established and well known. There is the casual meeting with promises to get together, the lunch date that ends with the invitation for dinner at the former student's house to show appreciation, the carefully cooked meal that leads to bed if the former student desires it, is previously lesbian, and does not have a live-in lover or a relationship with another student, former or otherwise. Then there is nothing else. Augusta likes to think of herself as a woman who does not flourish on the clutter of relationships; that is Tina's style, not her own.

The pool woman on the floor with Augusta for the first time and what Augusta knows will be the last time is very very tan and slight. Augusta imagines that even the pool woman's bones are tan, that the long humerus that juts through the pool woman's elbow into Augusta's stomach is not bleached white as it would have been had it been exposed to the sun without the cover of muscle and flesh. Instead, the pool woman's bones are a hot, sweet shade of brown, like bones that had been buried in rich, wet soil and tunneled by hungry insects. Or so August visualizes, as her own bones soften into flesh; as her own flesh solidifies into water.

It was before the two women had made love that the pool woman had vacuumed. Augusta had watched the pool woman's thin, muscled arms charm the long snakes of hose, wondering about the pool woman's childhood. She imagined that the pool woman came from a large family in Citrus or Orange county; that the pool woman grew up expecting to marry a man like her father who worked as a supervisor in the orange and grapefruit groves. Or perhaps the pool woman had grown up on the coast, in a city like St. Augustine, learning to surf better than her brother and dreaming of finding a mermaid in the waves. Augusta knew she would never ask the woman anything, even if she had sex with her: what if the woman was from someplace like Cincinnati?

Augusta sat in a lounge chair, studying the pool woman, the pool, and the gray wall, wondering how wet the pool woman became during sex, and pretending to read a minor novel by a minor woman who would never rise to the fame of an entry on a women's studies syllabus. Augusta always intended to devote her summers to discovering undiscovered women and to creating a course. But Augusta knew that as soon as she required her students to discover the woman, the woman was no longer undiscovered. Or, Augusta thought, she might create a totally new paradigm for teaching women's studies, something that transcended male-created disciplines like sociology and literature, transcended even male-defined categories like class and gender. But Augusta's summer never seemed long enough. It took months to bake and swim away the tension she collected during the academic year.

Tina indulged Augusta's lazy summers, perhaps even creating them by her insistence on purchasing this house. "Why the hell live in Florida and not have pool?" Tina had laughed. The house was inconveniently located, but no more so than almost every other house in the sprawling suburb of Orlando, which did not serve as a bedroom for a real city but as one for the fantasy world of tourist attractions. The house had no driveway, no trees in the front yard, and no character, but home ownership was vital to their view of themselves as a couple. It was also part of their view of themselves that Augusta was brilliant but brittle, and that Tina was a pragmatic caretaker. The caretaker was the one who convinced Augusta that she deserved to have a pool, although Tina herself could not swim. The caretaker was the one who prescribed nonmonogamy for Augusta's complexities, and Tina only engaged in it herself (or so she said) out of an excessive sense of fairness.

In the afternoon, after the pool woman is gone, Tina telephones the pool company to complain about the pool.

The pool has sediment on the bottom, sediment that the pool woman had promised would not reappear. It looks like a fine gray charcoal, like ashes sifted after a fire. The pool woman had explained to Augusta that the sediment was caused by a chemical reaction between the chlorine sticks and another compound she referred to by a splash of unrelated letters. Although Augusta could not remember the chemical's name, she remembered that it appeared on the service bill every month, remembered that it was white.

Augusta did not trust the pool woman's explanation because she did not trust chemistry: how could two virginally white substances combine to produce that sinister silt that shifted along the bottom of the pool?

♦

Augusta had never studied chemistry in school. Once she had wanted a chemistry set for Christmas. She and her best friend, Kathy Daniels, each asked their mothers for one.

What both of their mothers said was no, explaining that
their daughters could blow up the entire apartment building.
At first, both Augusta and Kathy thought that their mothers'
fear was an excuse. Later, the girls overheard their mothers,
best friends themselves, talking in one or the other of their
narrow kitchens, sitting over cooling coffee, Duncan Hines
chocolate cake, and cigarettes.

One mother had said, "Those girls could blow this entire
building to Kingdom Come."

The other mother answered, "Jesus," almost laughing,
but with a catch of fear deep in her smoke-filled throat.

The girls knew then that they would never be given
chemistry sets. What the girls did get, every June on the last
day of school when they brought home their final report
cards like passports to the country of the next grade, was a
summer pass to Beginni's Swim Club, around the corner
from their Newark, New Jersey apartment building. The
mothers bought these passes for their daughters, even if the
mothers could not afford luxuries for themselves, because
the passes were not luxuries. The passes kept the daughters
off of the hot summer streets that might provoke rioting and
out of the cool city stores that might prove tempting. The
mothers were trying to protect their daughters from laws
against breaching the peace and shoplifting; trying to protect
their daughters from additional juvenile convictions. The
mothers were also thinking that Beginni's Swim Club might
keep their daughters safe from boys for another summer.
The mothers had to work.

For several summers at Beginni's the girls persisted in the
magical safety purchased by their mothers. The girls held
hands and kissed underwater. If anyone ever noticed, the
observer thought of them not as potential sexual deviants
but as playful, young domesticated animals like kittens or
puppies. The girls thought of themselves more as dolphins
than kittens, and usually more as mermaids than as humans.
They swam with their ankles crossed and their legs pressed
tightly together. The chlorinated water rushing between their
thighs and through their bathing suit bottoms gave them
pleasure, but this pleasure was indistinct from other
pleasures of the body, such as opening their eyes underwater
or finally letting their lungs fill with air.

The mermaids were swimmers, but they also became adept at diving. They were coached by the lifeguards at Beginni's Swim Club and always entered into the Labor Day competitions which their mothers attended, cheering for their daughters. The lifeguards, who the girls thought of as *guys*, were doing daily laps between boyhood and manhood. These guys all had girlfriends upon whom they made sexual demands, although at least one of the guys was figuring out that he was more attracted to his fellow lifeguards than his girlfriend. But the guys were more boys than men when they coached the mermaids. The only lust that ever made one of these guys touch the mermaids was the passion for the perfect dive. A lifeguard's hand on one of the girls' buttocks meant she needed to tuck before springing into the water, nothing more.

If any other male approached the girls, the mermaids pretended that they could not speak English (or any other language in which the male might be fluent). The mermaids conversed in a cross between the dolphin squeaks they heard on the television program *Flipper*, and the Spanish, Yiddish, Russian, and Chinese they heard on the streets and within the walls of their own apartment building. Then they would swim underwater to a location upon which they had apparently agreed after much debate. If an unusual male was undeterred and pursued, he might find himself in the shadow of an overheated lifeguard who had decided to swim over to the girls with professionally menacing strokes. In the watery world of Beginni's Swim Club, the girls were as impervious to threats of rape as mermaids.

Their shimmering safety ended when the girls got older. It ended before the girls' bodies betrayed them with breasts promising a voluptuousness worthy of any mermaid, before the newly hired lifeguards started to think of them as potential girlfriends, before the girls abandoned the language they had created. It ended when the law allowed them to apply for working papers.

Those summers in the unairconditioned clothing warehouse heaving autumn wools and corduroy made Kathy Daniels crazy enough to marry the first man who promised her that she would never have to work again. Those same summers, and the lonely one after Kathy got married, and the ones that seemed the same after Kathy got divorced, made Augusta think. Augusta thought about Kathy, moving nearby to the almost-suburb of West Orange (or was it South Orange?) which, as Kathy reported, had not a single orange tree, although there were wonderful yards; and about Kathy moving back to the almost-slum of her mother's apartment which, as Kathy observed, at least did not house some man trying to suck at her as if she were full of sweet juice. Augusta thought about their mothers, working in the same warehouse, summers and winters and the seasons between.

Augusta thought about the women who would wear the heavy clothes she was picking for an order from a store in Oklahoma that would mark-up each item at least fifty percent; for an outlet in Idaho that sold second-quality merchandise and marked it up only forty-five percent. Augusta thought about women all the time. Certainly she thought about kissing them and being kissed by them, stroking them and being stroked by them, swimming with them in some body of water created solely for them. But Augusta also thought of women more abstractly. She thought of them in percentages of consumers who would choose the green wool pleated skirt over the blue plaid A-line. She thought of the women who would shoplift the lined winter coats. She thought of housewives reading novels and mistresses smoking cigarettes and girls who should be outside playing basketball but who fit themselves into kitchens to cook dinners. Sometimes she thought of women as chemicals capable of predictable reactions, if only she could discover the formula.

Augusta worked in the warehouse through high school, through college, through her Ph.D. in sociology at Rutgers. After the coursework and the dissertation ("Working Women in the Garment Trades, 1950–1965"), she quit the warehouse. After six years of teaching ("Women and Work," "The Literature of Working Women," "Women and the Economy"), she almost never thinks of the warehouse. She still thinks about women. She still thinks about sex with women. But she still mostly thinks about theoretical women, women who have no smell.

◆

Stretched on a lounger by the pool, Augusta's mind is filled with patterns as abstract as the design on her bathing suit. She is watching the wind blow the furry mimosa leaves across the too-low wall and into the water, when she sees the pool woman reappear through the gate. Augusta thinks that the pool woman is more narrow than she remembered, although it had only been this morning since the two women had tasted the faint spice of chlorine on each other's skin.

"You bitch," the pool woman hisses, walking on the deck toward Augusta.

"What's the matter?" Augusta asks, although she thinks she already knows. Augusta is a woman well trained in the danger of assumptions.

"The matter?" The pool woman sounds like an underwater echo, like Flipper reverberating in ultrasonic waves.

The pool woman comes closer. Augusta clumsily gets up from the lounger. She looks at her watch, fastened around her sandal. She hopes that Tina will keep her promise to be home late. Augusta would be more embarrassed to be caught in a scene than in an embrace.

"I'll tell you what's wrong. I got fired. I got fired because some damn dyke I serviced on her kitchen floor after I serviced her pool called up and complained that I left sediment on the bottom. 'The bottom of what?' I ask the boss, 'the bottom of her high and mighty ass or the bottom of her pool?' 'What do you think?' he says. And then the prick fires me."

"I didn't mean for you to get fired."

"Oh, how nice. And I'm going to be just as nice. I'm here to clean the sediment from the bottom of your pool with your damn ass."

Augusta wonders whether she should resist the tan woman rushing toward her with the long-handled pool broom. Part of Augusta would love to glide underwater with the pool woman's tanness, almost like making love again. Part of Augusta doesn't want to get her hair wet this late in the afternoon.

Augusta does not remember deciding. All she remembers when she wakes up wet on the cement next to the lounger is that the pool woman was here, but now she is gone. Augusta slips on her sandals. The watch clicks on the ground as she walks. Augusta checks the side gate, cursing the pool woman for not closing it, but she does not close it herself.

Instead, Augusta goes to the bedroom she shares with Tina. She towels her hair, but gets dressed without showering. She wears white cotton jeans, white sneakers, and a T-shirt she brought home for Tina from the ninth annual National Women's Studies Association conference. She wants to go and get a new piece of clothing, something light and summery. Something nice. Something that will make Tina want to take her out to dinner, no matter how late Tina gets home or where she has been.

Altamonte Mall, with its one hundred and six specialty shops and its five major department stores, floats in the middle of a whirlpool of traffic. Augusta is sucked safely to its center and finds an unshaded parking space identical to at least a thousand other slots painted onto the hot asphalt. Once this land had been devoted to groves, as Augusta knows from one of her published papers ("The Migrant Farmworker Woman in Florida: 1950–1965"). Augusta can picture the long rows of the popular Valencia and the profitable Hamlin orange trees, dotted with bulbs that would be rapidly abandoning their greenness at this time of year. Soon, a grower in tepid gray Sansabelt slacks would walk among the trees, watching a migrant woman dive from her ladder for ripe fruits. Augusta imagined the noble lines of movement rippling from the woman's work; the grower was only a space covered with clothes. The grower further proved his ignominious greed by selling the land to developers, an even more vacuously despicable breed. Augusta mourned the loss of work for the migrant woman, who probably would not fit the wholesome image required for even minimum-wage employment at any Magic Kingdom enterprise. Augusta does not think about the grower or the developer, except as conspirators to deprive all women of the sacred citrus groves. Augusta had never actually been in a grove, but she consoled herself that she had never been to Disney World either.

The mall is cool and crowded with people trying to escape the shimmering heat. Augusta remembers that her

mother always said that five o'clock was the hottest part of
the day. Augusta looks at the golden space on her arm where
her watch should have been. The building is filled with girls
mostly, Augusta notices; or perhaps Augusta notices only the
girls. The mall as municipal swimming pool, Augusta thinks,
as if it is the title of an article she read, or one she will think
about writing.

It is a pale green-blue, like reflected water. Light as a
ripple across protected water. Soft as skin underwater. It is a
blouse of washable silk. Affordable, really. On sale, even.
The credit cards wait patiently in Augusta's wallet, next to
the blank checks drawn on a joint account with a
comfortable balance.

Augusta expertly shoplifts the blouse. The thrill of the
threat of getting caught is mitigated by her professionalism.
In another store, she buys, with cash, a scarf for Tina.
Augusta never steals gifts.

She is glad when she sees Tina's Peugeot parked several
houses down, with a parking space conveniently in front of
it. As Augusta angles her car, she looks down at her new silk
blouse. She hopes she is not sweating in it. Still, seeing Tina's
car makes her glad that she changed into it at the mall
bathroom.

But Tina is not home. Does not come to the door like she
usually does. Or she is home, but hiding. They do not know
any neighbors. There is no place close enough to walk. She
must be home. Augusta checks the bedroom. Her sandals are
dry now, on the floor where she left them, the watch still
attached by its strap. Tina is not napping on the bed; she is
not in the bathroom where Augusta's swimsuit is draped on
the towel rack. Augusta walks into the kitchen. She pushes
past the garbage, slides open the glass door. Augusta enters
the fast twilight.

From the edge of the concrete deck, Augusta sees a
shadow. She squints at it. At first she thinks it is the
sediment, collected into a shapeless monster at the deep end
of the pool. She wonders if the shadow is too large to be one
woman's body, too large to be only Tina, too large to be
only the pool woman.

Augusta looks at the wall. She thinks about women:
about women's clothes, about women's work, about

women's childhoods. She thinks about women's bodies; about thinking, about breathing water, about waiting to be buoyed by death. Then she dives into the pool, her ankles crossing like the memory of a mermaid, her silk blouse clinging to the memory of air.

MERRY X-MAS

Jewelle Gomez

Trees dropped silently into the past as the Trailways bus rolled north on Interstate 95 toward Cape Cod. Lena loved riding buses. She could *feel* their voices—a low, soft natal rumble that lulled her almost to sleep. Two more hours and she'd be home again. For a brief moment she felt like Little Red Riding Hood: "To grandmother's house we go." But this time she went alone—no mother, sisters, or uncles. The past of her girlhood was alive inside her, but the future remained hidden in the darkness outside the grimy bus window.

In New York, a sense of separateness had weighed down on Lena. The wide, open world felt narrow and closed for her. Each day was an intellectual exercise in survival. Her life became a therapeutic theory that proved she could fit in with a crowd and still feel alone.

At night she'd cried, disappointed at the seats too often left empty beside her. And she felt cheated. Lena could not be comforted by the sound of her own sobs. Her tears would spread like silent, hot candle wax inside of her, then cool, locking her in a grip of fear. What had the struggle been for? Why had she made her way to the city and then shut down? "Even if I could hear," she thought, "I'd be too afraid to speak."

And then her grandmother died, leaving Lena completely alone. But she had left Lena the house in Oak Bluffs. Left it to her and her younger sister. Sometimes they came up together for vacations, but now that her sister was engaged, those visits were less and less. This weekend Lena came alone, not sure what she wanted except to get away from the noise of people she could not hear, friends she could not find.

Lena closed her eyes in the bus and saw the front porch of MaDear's house. She could smell the sea in the air and almost feel the tide pulling and pushing her. She could hear the high-pitched squawk of the sea gulls like sharp points pricking the skin on the back of her neck. She thought about her grandmother, MaDear, tall and thin, the deep black of her skin rich against the red kerchief she seemed to always have around her neck. It grew dark with the sweat of cleaning or cooking or sitting in the sun and then was periodically replaced with its spitting image, bright and crisp. MaDear had been her ally and her haven. She'd been the first in the family to study the signs so she could talk to little Lena. When Lena understood that the white children in the after-school program for the deaf were making fun of her, MaDear was the only one she could tell, since her mother didn't want her going to the program at all. MaDear had been the only one who didn't make her feel that being deaf was a curse that might be catching. MaDear. And Merry.

Lena smiled, remembering her childhood dream. Every summer she'd spent with MaDear she played in the attic after supper, amongst the old furniture, clothes, and family albums. A large old painting always sat on an oak dresser: six women in vintage bathing clothes digging for clams on the beach. One was looking back impudently over her shoulder as she kneeled in the sand. Lena had called her Merry. The others, who remained unnamed, played at the edge of the waves or walked holding hands. All of them smiled in a way that drew Lena back to the picture each year. She could not stay away.

Christmas was Lena's favorite holiday. The spicy smells and sparkling lights always excited her, as if something truly special were about to happen. And it did: MaDear always came in from the Cape to spend the holiday week with Lena and the rest of the family in the city. Christmas, MaDear, and the Cape were all so special to her. So in the cottage, Lena decided that the woman in the picture with the impudent smile needed a name. Merry was it.

Merry became Lena's friend, growing up with her each year. Sometimes Lena would fall asleep on the upholstered settee and dream that Merry spoke to her out loud. She would hear her say, "Lena, little Lena," as clear as all of those other sounds she never heard. Lena always ran upstairs anxiously to greet her, afraid Merry would not answer any more. But she did every year until MaDear died and Lena became too grown up and Cape Cod summers became occasional.

When Lena finally opened the front door of the small cottage, then locked it behind her, she saw it looked the same as it had when last she left. She stretched the bus-ride kinks out of her legs and snatched the dust covers from the tables, lamps, and chairs. She dusted quickly, making the old mahogany shine, and plumped the pillows so they looked inviting rather than abandoned. Soon it felt like her grandmother's home again. *MaDear's.*

Moon shadows played over the ceiling, bouncing off the four-poster bed as Lena put on fresh sheets. The New England night was thick and damp. Lena thought about wood for the fireplace and decided to wait until the next day. She crawled into her bed, remembering how good it had felt to be fourteen years old in MaDear's house. How safe she had felt. But now, alone in the dark and the silence she felt a quick chill of fear. *There could be sounds out there waiting to hurt her.* She closed that thought out and pulled the covers to her. The room was much the same as it had been for the past twenty years. She looked around the darkness and tried to recognize its familiarity. Finally, she closed her eyes and dreamed about the seagulls she might hear in the morning.

The next day Lena fixed a picnic of canned goods: sardines and olives and a Thermos of tea. She went up to the attic where it was quite warm, but mustier than the rest of the house. Sunlight washed over the stored furniture, showing up the dust. The picture was still there. It was sitting on a dresser that had no knobs and one short leg. Lena sat down and looked at it as she ate.

It was done in oil by a studied hand. The strokes were smooth yet short, giving the impression that the summer heat really rose from the sand. The women's clothes were caught by an unseen wind, firming the outline of their hips and breasts. Merry was still there in the painting. She looked up with the same quizzical glance from the canvas. Now she seemed older than when Lena was last here. Lena curled up on the settee and felt her tears drop onto the brocade fabric. With the tears came release from anxiety. This was her home and she was happy to be at here. The world outside of Cape Cod was put in its proper perspective. She closed her eyes and slept. Then she heard a voice.

"Lena, little Lena." Whispered, light.

She struggled up from sleep, but could not seem to open her eyes. Her heart was pounding, but she did not know what there might be to fear. She shook her head as if to clear her head of the voice.

"Lena, little Lena." Louder, stronger.

Then hands clutched at her, pulling at her clothes, at her short, natural-cut hair. It felt as if one hand was holding her mouth closed. She fought to scream. Her scream remained in her throat, choking her, making her cough against the firm hand she could not dislodge. She clawed at the air and jerked herself up, eyes open now. She stared into the brightly lit room, where nothing was disturbed—no outstretched hands, no intruder. Then she heard a voice say her name. Heard it.

"Lena." She looked at the painting. It had been a while since she'd last been here. But the painting seemed the same—the colors maybe just a little brighter. Lena noticed that one of the bathers was wearing a brightly colored necklace and then heard her name again. She blinked and stared at the painting, searched the attic room, blinked again, shut her eyes tightly for a moment. Lena's terror pushed up through her stomach, surging up to her throat. Then it was her own hand holding the scream inside.

This can't be, Lena thought, *This is my dream. Dreams aren't real*. She ran from the attic, bolting the door. She stood trembling at the foot of the stairs for a moment as if listening, but as usual there was nothing. She ran out of the house, down to the beach and sat in the damp sand when she could not run anymore. Lena watched the waves struggle

in and drift out again. Everything was as it usually was on
Cape Cod in the spring. Except she'd run from the only
place she really called home and had run as far as she could.
Where could she go now? Only the ocean lay before her and
an empty, noisy city behind. She looked back at the house,
MaDear's house, the house she loved, its open windows and
curtains blowing in the breeze and inviting her back.

Lena thought about her teaching job, her little
apartment, her soon-to-be-married sister, her divorced
mother. She thought about all of the feelings she'd been too
embarrassed to express, too ashamed to be the dummy in a
world that could not hear her. That had never happened to
her here.

She walked back to the house and threw the folded
sheets over the high-winged chair, the mahogany dining table
and the rolltop desk. She unpacked and stored her suitcase,
then went up to the attic. She stopped only an instant before
unbolting the door. She looked backward down the stairs
and smiled.

When Lena opened the attic door, sun still washed the
room but from a slightly steeper angle, making the light soft,
putting the painting in shadow. She saw the bathers and
realized that one wore not a necklace but a bright scarf
around her neck.

Her friend Merry was not there!

Lena looked into the shadow and saw Merry standing
beside the painting. Merry stepped forward and stood beside
the settee where the sun was still bright. Lena saw her
clearly—her sun-bleached hair, her arms brown with the
days at the canvas shore. Then she closed the attic door
behind her.

Merry's hands danced in the air, the words coming fast,
*Come with me. We'll never be apart again. We've waited so
long.*

Lena didn't respond, only stared in amazement and tried
to calm the pounding of her heart. She looked back to the
painting, slowly recognizing the distant figure, tall and thin.
Merry went on, knowing that Lena would need time to
recover in order to speak.

"Don't you like to dig for clams?" Merry asked her.

"I think so," Lena said in a quavering voice, "It's been a long time."

"Will you come with me? Be with us?" Merry asked, reaching out to Lena. Merry's hands were dark and a few tiny grains of sand glistened in the hairs on her arm.

Lena nodded and Merry smiled like the sunrise.

"I missed you. We all missed you."

Lena looked at the painting where five women stooped in the sand, and she smiled, a full, deep smile, for the first time in many years.

Lena started to speak, but Merry held her hands gently, as the sun moved through the sky behind and beyond the women.

Shadow finally enveloped the room. The painting sat firmly on the dresser where it had been for many years. In it, seven women dug for clams in the sand, laughing together. Silently.

THE TREE

Ellen S. Korr

Today was Sarah's birthday. It was the first time in seventy-nine years she had celebrated it alone. As her head nodded to the rhythmic breathing, it matched the rocking of the chair in which she sat. A bit of yellow-white hair hung down her forehead as her chin rested on her chest. Time had aged her face and hands, but these lines could not hide the air of grace and beauty that lay beneath the surface.

The vision she sees before her is of a woman lying in a hospital bed. Clear plastic tubes flow from her nose, around her neck, past her ear, then travel to the wall. Wires of black and red spin busy little webs to a monotonous beeping machine of green and yellow lines. Intravenous tubes stream from both hands, and two thick catheter tubes break the smoothness of the worn white blanket.

This is Rachael, the woman Sarah had loved for over forty-seven years. This is what is left of a lifetime of living and loving together.

The woman's lips, cracked and pale, quiver a last message. Sarah moves in closer to hear the words.

"I promise you . . . something special . . . on your birthday," she says in labored breath.

"Don't try to talk, honey, save your strength," Sarah whispers in return.

The machine screams a straight line and Rachael expels her last breath.

Sarah opened her eyes with a start, not wanting to relive the rest of the dream again.

A warm breeze gently blew the edge of Sarah's skirt. Brilliant sunlight accompanied a songbird's melody as they rolled through the window, bringing her back to the present day.

The clock on the mantel chimed its soft strokes three times, echoing through the sunroom off the kitchen.

"Oh! It's time," she said, as she turned toward the sound.

She turned her head to look out the window; her eyes strayed to the large old tree in the back yard. She had watched its growth for the past forty years with her lover. But for the past eight months she had stared at the tree alone.

The tree's limbs spread out like arms reaching to envelope the world. Some of the thick, low branches, only a few inches above the rich lush grass, grew horizontally to reach out and stretch and touch the ground, and then turned again to extend their tiny limbs to the sky. The tree's unique body had many low, level places where one could easily sit comfortably to enjoy the summer air and sunshine. A secondary trunk stretched out horizontally away from the main trunk at sitting height. It reached a full thirty feet long at its longest point. Smaller branches grew straight down into the ground to support its weight all along its lengthy path.

Eager to go sit in her tree, Sarah rose with the aid of her cane and slowly headed for the back door. She had performed this ritual since the passing of her beloved Rachael and found inner peace alone being near the place where they had spent so much time together over the decades.

Sarah and Rachael had fallen in love with the tree the first time they saw it. To them it had been one of the selling points of the house. They chatted about all the parties and picnics they could have under the tree, as the realtor tried to urge them back into the house to show them the upstairs. Rachael gave Sarah a wink and they knew then the house was theirs and this would become their own private little world, their heaven.

Precise, tiny steps carried Sarah slowly down the well-worn path on the gentle slope toward the tree. She stopped by a tiny tea rose bush to pick a single perfect bud just blooming.

"I'm coming, my love. I'll be there in just a little while," she said aloud, as she breathlessly ambled closer to the tree. Her gait was slow but steady. Nearing the tree, she walked past one of the two heavy metal chairs in which she normally sat and reached out to brace herself on one of the lower branches. She then clutched one of the upright limbs as if she were hugging someone.

"I'm here, darling," she said softly, breathing rapidly. "Let me just catch my breath and I'll be right with you," she spoke into the afternoon summer light.

She placed her cane in the crook of a lower limb and proceeded toward a branch shaped much like a chair. She turned carefully to get more comfortable on her shaded seat and leaned back on a somewhat upright branch. Carefully she put the tiny rosebud in the crevice of a nearby branch. She put her two arms on other branches, as if she were sitting in a recliner. Sarah took a deep breath and expelled it with a big sigh.

"Ah, that's better, now I'm ready," she said to herself.

Relaxed in her perched position she remembered the days when she wasn't alone in the tree. As in her regular visits to the tree she could also feel the silent presence of her lover. Ever so subtly the familiar fragrance of Rachael's perfume reached her nostrils.

"How I love your smell," she said aloud, breathing in slowly and deliberately. Sarah always talked to Rachael with never any response. But she always knew Rachael was either near or by her side in the tree. Sarah stretched and looked at her hands. Slowly the wrinkles started to disappear.

"Keep your eyes closed," a voice said, "I'm going to do something different this time."

Her heart skipped a beat. That voice. It was Rachael. There was definitely no mistaking that. Sarah kept her eyes closed as she felt movement on a branch beside her. This was a new sensation. She felt small delicate fingers caress her face. She reached up and put her arms around a warm, clothed body and held it firmly.

"Oh, you're really here this time!" Sarah whispered, feeling Rachael's lips caress her face, neck, then shoulder.

Sarah felt Rachael's lips travel slowly back to her neck and lips and then to her throat. Tiny tongue licks and kisses moved down between her breasts as Rachael nestled her face against Sarah's breast. When Sarah's eyes opened she saw her beloved Rachael, and the flame-red hair that flowed down the youthful body she remembered so well through the years. She wore the same white cotton blouse and plaid pleated skirt she had worn when they first met.

"Sarah, yes, I'm really here," Rachael said. "I told you I'd have a birthday present for you."

Sarah released her embrace. She looked at her arms and felt her face.

"Oh, Rachael! Look at my arms, they're so smooth, and my face feels so young again! My hands have no wrinkles either!"

"Of course. You're young. You'll always be young to me." Joyfully, Rachael stroked Sarah's blonde hair and continued to shower her with kisses.

"I always loved these precious times with you under the tree," Sarah paused, "And now that you're really here, you make me feel so strong and full of life again."

"Hush now, my love," Rachael whispered between kisses, "no more talking." She softly muffled any sound coming from Sarah's lips. Then Rachael kissed Sarah's brow and each eyelid, her cheeks, nose, and chin. Rachael's tongue lightly touched Sarah's throat and the lovely valley between her breasts. Sarah and Rachael's clothes seem to fade before them as agile fingers stroked Sarah's bare shoulders and arms. Rachael gently cupped her lover's breasts in her hand and then leaned over to kiss them both. She pulled Sarah close so bare flesh pressed together. Then Rachael slid her body down the tree to move her kisses down past Sarah's breasts to her belly. The soft summer breeze cooled Sarah's bare body as Rachael continued on her quest. Sarah sighed her contentment as Rachael's travels brought her to Sarah's inner thigh and slowly up to her velvet pearl. As a diver submerges beneath the surface, so did Rachael. Relentlessly she pursued Sarah, searching for the precious pearl. Surfacing and submerging with the continual rhythm of combing, probing, and teasing; diving, surfacing, and dipping. Time after time Rachael breathed in the essence of Sarah, taunting, prolonging, exploring, feeling her swell then drop with the rush of tongue and touch. Moment after moment the currents and streams within Sarah were pulsing and crashing like the swells of the tides along a shoreline until she could hold back no longer and the picture in her mind exploded into tiny lights as she remembered one similar night on a beach with Rachael on the Fourth of July. Warmth suffused Sarah's whole being as she reached for Rachael's arms, turned to kiss the face before her.

Rachael picked up the rosebud that Sarah had set aside earlier and held it to her lips.

"It always has such a strong fragrance," she said to Sarah. "Do you remember the day we planted it?"

"Our first fight." Sarah smiled.

She remembered the day nearly fifty years earlier. It was the first summer after they had moved into their new home. Sarah had pulled into the driveway in her brand new '52 Ford Fairlane convertible. She carried a small potted plant into the living room. "Rachael, honey, I'm home," she called out. "Look what I bought!"

"I'm out back," was the reply.

Sarah hummed a little tune as she opened the back door. Rachael stood with a garden hose in her hand, washing the grass clippings off the push mower. Rachael's long red hair was tied back with a scarf. Her face was smudged with green, and sweat dripped from it. She had wet marks under her arms, twigs and grass clippings on her cuffed shorts, and mud on her sneakers.

"Three hours to do the front and back. I can't take much more of this. We've got to save up for a gas-powered mower. Maybe we can even buy a rider." Rachael rattled on, barely looking at Sarah as she finished her cleanup.

"Mr. Jenkins at the nursery said I'm the first to have one." Sarah said, holding up the tiny tea rose plant. "They're imported from England." It displayed buds no bigger than her fingernail.

"I sent you for groceries." Rachael's tired voice begged. "How much did it cost? You know we're on a tight budget."

"I had enough left over from the shopping to get it."
Sarah said, unsure of herself now. "It was only $4.95."

"That could have been used as a down payment for a
new mower." The sweat glistened off Rachael's face and
chest from the heat bearing down from the mid-afternoon
sun. "And where are the groceries? Ice cream was on your
list. It's probably soup now."

Sarah's eyes filled with tears as she ran back into the
house. "I just wanted to surprise you with something pretty."

Sarah had just finished storing the last of the groceries
away in the kitchen when Rachael entered, freshly showered.
She hesitated before approaching the still tearful Sarah.

"Honey, we've got to talk." Rachael said firmly. "Stop
crying and look at me."

Tears flooded Sarah's eyes again. She couldn't bear any
more of Rachael's harsh words. Everything had been fine
until they moved into the house. Tension had crept up on
them there. It wasn't what Sarah had hoped for. Rachael put
her hand on Sarah's shoulder.

"Sarah, I love you."

Sarah slowly lifted her head to face the concern in
Rachael's amber eyes. The love she had always known in
those eyes twinkled back at her.

"I love you, too." Sarah whispered.

"You know how hard it was to get this house. I don't
want us to fail. Not even at the smallest things." Rachael's
voice was calm but soft. "You manage hundreds of
thousands of dollars for the Acme Press. If it weren't for
your accounting skills, that company would have gone under
last year. I don't manage money, but I manage people and
supplies at the hospital. In my business, progress is made
with teamwork. So, all I'm saying is we must plan these
things, together."

"I'm sorry, you're right. I should have . . ."

". . . could have gone and picked out the plant,
together?" Rachael insisted.

"You're so right. I . . . "

"I think we should go plant this little bush together,"
Rachael said, kissing away the last of Sarah's tears.

When the planting was finished, they sat under the tree making promises of sharing and deciding their future together.

Now, they sat together again on this special birthday of Sarah's under their beloved old tree. They held each other for the rest of the afternoon. Caressing, kissing, talking, and sharing other stories of the past. They sat under the tree and watched the sun slowly burn to a magnificent fireball sunset.

"Darling, you'd better get dressed, now. It's almost dark," Rachael told her lover.

Reluctantly, Sarah lowered herself to the ground to retrieve her clothes piled at the foot of the tree. While Sarah dressed, Rachael stroked Sarah's hair. Rachael moved down to the lowest part of the tree to be level with Sarah and leaned forward to kiss her. Their kiss was a long and passionate one. Then Rachael gently pushed Sarah away.

"I'll come for you one more time, tomorrow. Then nothing will ever separate us again. I love you."

"You promise?" Sarah heard the age creeping into her voice.

"Absolutely." Rachael kissed her softly. "Now you'd better get going."

"You're right, I must get in the house before dark. I love you too," Sarah said, and turned to start up the slope.

"Don't forget your cane."

Sarah reached for the cane reluctantly.

At the back door Sarah turned and waved, with both hands, to Rachael. The cane above her head and the other hand slowly moving back and forth toward the one she loved. Rachael waved back, still seated in the tree.

When Sarah turned again to reach for the door knob she saw her hand was old and wrinkled, and the weight of her years fell heavily upon her again.

Slowly, with a sigh, she walked to her rocking chair and sat. From the west window there was still just enough light to see the silhouette of the tree. As she turned to peer out to her beloved tree she saw that no one was in it. She then said aloud, in her tiny aged voice, as if it could be heard a great distance, "Tomorrow, my love, I'll be with you, tomorrow."

She closed her eyes, the image of the tree spread before her, its limbs wide, like the arms of her lover.

WEEPING WILLOWS

Joanne Dahme

On most of the summer nights last year, Joey and I were hiking across the humped graves of the old Willows Cemetery. Joey's dad died last summer, just three weeks after Joey's thirteenth birthday. And ever since the day of the funeral, Joey wanted to go there, where his dad was buried. It was a weird way to spend the summer, but our visits became a ritual. More Joey's ritual than mine, but Joey was my best friend, so every day last summer that's where we'd be.

Joey acted like he didn't have anywhere else to go. At least he didn't seem interested in doing anything else. At first it didn't seem so weird. I mean, if he wanted to be close to his dad, or maybe to say goodbye without all of his aunts and relatives pushing up against him, well, the cemetery was where to find Mr. Daly. I figured, if it had been my dad, I probably wouldn't have been able to get it out of my mind either. But after awhile, I got really worried. When I asked Joey about it, about why he had to go to the cemetery every night, he said he didn't want to forget his dad, like so many other people already seemed to be doing. He said even his mom had started to act normal again, cleaning the house, cooking dinner—like his dad had never even been there. I didn't know what to say to change his mind. I figured maybe it was just something he had to do for a while.

And Joey was my best friend. It just seemed natural that I went along with him.

It was the same every night. After dinner, we'd meet on the bridge in the park where the summer before we had caught so many crayfish, or "crawdaddies" as Joey called them. We used to spend hours wading through the cool stream, lifting rocks and plunging our hands into the slimy gravel beneath them. Last summer though, when Joey's dad died, we didn't even think about the crayfish. We just met there, since it was close to both of us and on the way to the cemetery. Sometimes we didn't even talk for a while. It didn't seem that we really needed any words. After all, we both knew where we were going and what we were going to do there. We just met to run across the ballfield, to scale the fence and climb onto the railroad tracks without even looking, because we could always hear the train coming, and besides, we pretty much knew the train schedule from habit. They usually came by every hour, not always at the same time, but at least an hour apart to pass through Oak. The trains always slowed as they came through town, like they didn't want to make too much noise and wake everyone up or something. We'd follow the tracks until we were crossing the railroad bridge, which shimmied up to the far north end of the cemetery. From the bridge we just slid down the gravel and stone embankment into the cemetery. Of course, we could have always just walked through the front gate of the cemetery. They were never closed that early in the summer. But Joey never felt right about doing it. The gates looked so official. Maybe because he didn't like to admit that his dad was really there.

Joey's dad was buried on the south end, about a fifteen-minute walk from our drop off. We walked in silence, crossing through the rows and rows of white tombstones. They were lined up so well they made us dizzy, so that when we walked, we would look at our feet so as not to notice. Besides, we were always careful not to tread over the mounds that rose at the base of the stones, especially if the ground looked new and without grass. But the birds and the whippoorwills made up for our silence, so that the cemetery never seemed really quiet. At the funeral everyone had been whispering, even crying in a whispery sort of way. The birds and the bugs seemed to be yelling in comparison. Both Joey and I liked that. He said that his dad always talked about how the summer noises made him happy. Once or twice Joey brought a radio so his dad could listen to the ballgame, but it just didn't sound right out there.

It was easy to spot Mr. Daly's grave, even from a hundred yards. His tombstone still looked clean and white, like bleached socks, especially from the back, but at least it didn't take long for the grass to grow on the mound. I hated seeing the plain brown dirt, even after it finally settled so that we weren't afraid to step on it or press against it with our hands. The dirt upset Joey. It scared me. At least with grass on it I didn't have to imagine the body underneath.

Mr. Daly's grave was in a nice spot too. He was toward the end of the row, not far from the south fenceline. On the other side of the fence was what was left of the woods, which sloped down to the river. The creek that passed through the park cut through the cemetery only two rows in front of Mr. Daly, and the vines of some of the big, beautiful willow trees that grew along the creek always looked like they were floating, even without any noticeable breeze. I liked looking at the willows bowing toward Mr. Daly. When I mentioned this to Joey, he smiled at me for the first time since his dad had died.

Every night had seemed the same, up until the night of the lightning storm. We both felt strangely right there, as if we belonged, sitting cross-legged by Mr. Daly's grave. Joey, keeping his dad's memory alive; me keeping my eye on Joey. It was as if we both had a summer job there or something. Joey would bring stuff to read, like mystery or war books from his dad's bookshelves. But Joey's favorite book that summer was a book he got from the library, stuff on reincarnation and spirits and stuff that made me kind of nervous. Joey knew how I felt about the book, but I couldn't make him give it up.

So that's how things went that summer, in the heat and the silence of the cemetery, by ourselves, until the night when the lightning turned the twilight sky into a flashbulb. It was early July, right after the fourth, on a day that had been so hot and sticky that Joey's mom let him skip basketball clinic that afternoon. I skipped with him. It was a weird day, the kind of day where you felt like something was going to happen, like something prickly in the air almost makes you move slow, slow enough not to disturb anything. We hung out at Joey's house the rest of the afternoon until dinner. After we ate, we headed out to the cemetery, Joey with his book tucked under his arm, even though the sky was already dark with fat black rain clouds.

By the time we reached Mr. Daly's grave, the wind was riffling through the willows like crazy. Together, the line of willows made a lot of noise, like they were waving us home, trembling at the approaching storm. No sooner had Joey and I gotten there, standing stiff against the wind, than a soft blowing rain began to fall.

It had rained a few times before, but only once did it rain hard enough that we couldn't wait it out beneath the branches of the willows. But this time the willows didn't look so protective. I turned from the trees to Joey to say, "Well, what do you say we go back?" He sort of shrugged. It was then that I noticed his brown hair was sort of floating toward the sky, almost like antennae. "Joey, geez, your hair, it's . . ."

Problem was, Joey started to point toward mine.

Then we heard the blast. Actually we felt the blast. It was so loud and so close that we both sort of instinctively dropped to the ground. For a moment, everything was light. It was like the light and the noise were pushing us to the ground. By the time we stood up, it was pouring. The rain suddenly felt so hard and so cold.

We both saw the wisps of smoke at the same time. It was about 500 yards in front of us, toward the middle of the cemetery.

"The lightning must have hit a tree!" Joey yelled to me, although I was right beside him.

"Come on!" I yelled back.

We ran through the rows of tombstones, without even a goodbye to Mr. Daly. The pelting rain had already made the grass and ground soft and squishy. Puddles lay between some of the graves. We ran through them.

Sure enough, one of the pine trees that seemed to just spring up in the cemetery had been hit. Its blackened side was still smoking. A clump of branches lay singed in a pile on the ground. I was so busy staring at the tree that I didn't notice the body laying not too far away, until Joey grabbed my arm.

"Look," he whispered.

It was a man. He lay wet and sprawled out, his face toward the sky. Joey and I gripped one another as we slowly moved toward him for a closer look. For minutes, we didn't do anything but stare at him. He didn't seem real to me, or I guess to Joey either, seeing Joey's look of amazement. The guy looked like he was sleeping, except that his skin was a funny color, almost gray, and still slightly smoking. Or was it just the mist from the rain? His mouth was slightly open and funny, gurgling sounds were coming from it. His pants were dirty. His white shirt and jacket were torn at his chest. He wasn't wearing any shoes, and his socks had holes in the bottom by the heels.

The scary part was, he looked a little like Mr. Daly. He was about the same age. He had dark hair, just like Joey's, except he was bald at the top, and the rest needed a cut. And he probably hadn't shaved for days. He smelled like the smoky bars that Joey's older brother Mike sometimes stopped in to pick up a six-pack when he was taking care of Joey.

"Joey," I tugged insistently at his sleeve. "Come on. We've got to tell somebody."

Joey knelt by the body, reaching out as if to touch it.

"No!" I yelled. I don't know why I yelled it. But Joey didn't look surprised.

"He looks like, a little bit . . . ," Joey started to say.

"No he doesn't. He doesn't. Let's go. We've got to tell somebody." I pulled him up. Joey looked at me.

"What's the matter?"

"What's the matter?" I repeated. "This guy just got struck by lightening! We have to get help." Joey was in a daze, but he didn't argue as I pulled him in the direction of the entrance gate. I wanted us out of there as fast as possible.

By the time we reached the gate, the rain had slowed to a misty drizzle. Parts of the street were a little bit flooded, so the cars were moving along like they didn't want to make a splash. We had been standing in the driveway for a few minutes when I saw an Oak police car coming over the hill.

"Hey!" I yelled, waving my arms and running to the edge of the driveway. "Stop!" Joey came up behind me, but he wasn't waving. Just sort of standing there, his eyes on the police car.

The car pulled into the driveway, right up beside us. The officer rolled down his window. He was older, like he could have been somebody's grandfather. He looked like he didn't want to get wet. "What's the problem, boys?" he asked sort of impatiently.

"There's a body in the cemetery, sir. We think it got struck by lightning," I answered quickly.

"A body?" he sounded suspicious. "Get into the car and show me." He pointed to the back seat, and Joey and I slid in.

"Aren't you one of the Daly kids?" he asked Joey as he peered at us in the rear view mirror. He was taking his time driving through the cemetery.

"Yes," Joey answered. Joey looked a little mad. Through all of this he still had that book with him. It was on his lap now, and he kept opening and closing the cover, making a flapping noise. I nudged him to stop.

"I'm sorry about your dad. I met him a few times. Seemed like a good man."

Joey only nodded. The book's cover was going up and down.

"There's the spot," I interrupted. From the driveway, we all could see the burnt tree. It wasn't smoking anymore.

I was the first one out of the car and ran to the spot where the body had been. It wasn't there anymore.

"Joey," I yelled over my shoulder. "Joey, he's gone!"

Now Joey ran up too. He didn't say a word. Just stared.

As the officer approached, I turned, like the words were pouring out of me to explain. He too was staring at the spot I was pointing to.

"He was there, sir. Joey and I both saw him. He was old, but not real old. He had dark hair, he looked a bit like . . ." and there I stopped. Joey at least was nodding in agreement.

"See," I continued, "You can see where he was lying in the

grass. See where the grass is a little flattened, like an outline
of someone lying there?"

The officer didn't say anything. He just sort of walked
around the area, looked at the tree, and bent down to pick
something up. It was a black shoe, with a hole right through
the bottom.

"Okay boys. Back in the car. Don't worry. We'll check
this out. But first I'm going to take you two home."

♦

I didn't sleep well that night. When I went to Joey's
house the next morning, he was sitting in the kitchen, poking
his spoon into a bowl of Cheerios. The bags under his eyes
looked darker then usual, so I guessed he had had problems
sleeping too.

"Joey, this is really weird. What do you think happened
to the guy?"

Joey didn't answer at first. He looked like he was
thinking, deciding on something. Then he turned to the
counter and grabbed the book lying next to the toaster. He
plopped *Specters and Ghosts: The Walking Dead* onto the
kitchen table. Then he looked me in the eye and waited, like
he was daring me to say something. I couldn't believe it.

"Joey, no way. You don't believe that stuff. I mean
reading about it doesn't make it true."

Joey played with his cereal some more before he
answered. "You saw him too, Danny. Dead bodies just don't
get up and walk away—unless they're not ready to be dead."

"That's crazy," was all I could answer. I was getting
nervous now. I was afraid for Joey. Afraid of what he might
be thinking. I reached for the book. I wanted to throw it out
the window or something, like, if I could get rid of the book,
I'd have the old Joey back.

Joey was too quick though when it came to that book.
His hand slapped down on mine, hard. "We have to go back
there, Danny. Now. Otherwise, we'll never be sure."

I just stared at him, pulling my hand out from under his.
It was stinging a little. "Okay, let's go." I was surprised to
hear the anger in my voice. When I think about it now, I
guess maybe I was just disappointed. Like, I was hanging out

with Joey all this time to make him feel better about his dad being dead, at least to help him accept it. And now this body shows up in the cemetery, giving Joey all kinds of scary ideas. I wanted it all to end.

We practically ran all the way to the cemetery. We even went through the front gate, since it was the shortest route to where the dead guy had been last night. The cemetery looked like a completely different place. The day was super bright, like all the rain in the world was gone. All of the birds were chirping like crazy. The only sign of the storm was tree branches, some of them pretty big, that were lying all over the place.

When we got to the spot where we had found the dead guy, Joey and I stopped for a minute to stare. I tried to imagine the scene from last night. Now though, even the grass where the dead guy had been lying had already sprung back to normal. But at least the tree was still black on its side. We both started looking close at the ground, kind of crouching to see if we could find anything. It was while we were checking the tree out that we heard his voice.

"You boys looking for something?"

The two of us whipped around so fast that we nearly collided. The dead guy was leaning, almost sitting, right on top of a tombstone just a few yards away. His face was still real pale, his hair wild. His clothes were dirty and rumpled, but dry now. But his eyes were shining. We hadn't gotten to see his eyes last night.

Neither of us said anything at first. I kept looking around the cemetery to see if anybody else was there, in case we needed help.

But I didn't see anyone. And you couldn't see the street from where we were. We were right in the center.

For a while we just stared. Finally Joey asked quietly, "Where did you go?"

"I'm not sure," the dead guy answered slowly. He sounded a little out of it, groggy. He was holding a shaky hand to his head. "One minute I was running toward the trees, and the next thing I remember is lying on the ground. I felt so hot and numb. I crawled all the way to the creek," he pointed in the direction of the southeast fenceline. "Wet my face," he kind of chuckled, maybe cause he thought about how wet he had already been. "Then I sort of crawled over to the willows. Guess I slept."

Joey was looking in the direction of his dad's grave. The dead guy slowly walked a tombstone closer to us.

"What are you doing here?" I interrupted. I felt nervous as hell. It took everything I had not to take a step back from him.

"I'm just passing through. Just been down on my luck lately, looking for a good place to settle." He shifted his weight. I noticed he still didn't have any shoes on.

"Where are your shoes, and what about your clothes?" I asked suspiciously. Nobody I know goes out without their shoes on.

He looked like he was trying to remember something. Then he looked a bit surprised.

"I don't know," he said finally. "Guess it doesn't matter," he barely spoke, nodding to himself.

"Where are you going now?" Joey asked, real quiet and concerned. He was staring hard at the dead guy's eyes.

"I have some friends beyond here," he answered slowly, "if I can catch up to them." He paused, as if thinking. And then added, "I really need to get out of here."

"Are you hungry?" Joey asked, almost hopeful, plunging his hand into his pocket like he was looking for money. He looked over at me, his eyebrows stern. I checked my pockets.

The dead guy slowly shook his head. "That's okay. I don't need it."

For a moment, Joey just stood there, like he was wrestling with a bunch of ideas. Then he said, kind of sadly, "We'll help you get out of here." Something in the way Joey said it made me keep my mouth closed.

Like I said before, we knew the train schedules. Joey, the dead guy, and I walked over to the embankment, a little beyond the bridge so we could get some flat ground along the tracks. Within fifteen minutes we saw the freight coming, slow and lumbering as usual. Joey had me lie near one of the rails, like I twisted my ankle or something and couldn't move.

As soon as we saw it approaching the bridge, Joey started waving his arms and yelling. "Stop! Stop! My friend is hurt!" He jumped onto the tracks and started running to meet the train. The train was already slowing and its brakes were screeching with the effort, but still I got scared with Joey running at it like that.

"Joey!" I screamed.

Joey stopped, then turned toward me, jogging over like he needed to point to exactly where I was. The train stopped far away enough that I didn't have to move from my spot. I could see the engineer leaning out of his cab, waving one of his guys in my direction. Joey stood beside me now. I looked up to catch his smile and looked in the direction of what he was smiling about.

The dead guy was scrambling up the embankment, kind of sloppily since he didn't have any shoes on. I thought of how the stones must be killing his feet, but he didn't seem to notice. When he got to the tracks and level ground he headed toward the back of the train. It didn't take him long to find a freight car with an open door. These trains always had some freights with their doors open. He hoisted himself up, and stopped for a moment to just look at us. He didn't wave or anything. Didn't even smile. Just looked, like he was memorizing us. I swear I could see his eyes shining from where I was. And then he was in.

♦

After that we didn't go to the cemetery every night anymore. Just once in a while, like to pay a visit. By the end of that summer, we weren't going at all. Joey started acting like his dad wasn't buried in there anyway. Like his dad had simply moved to another place where Joey couldn't follow him. But Joey seemed to understand. Even now, when someone who doesn't know Joey well asks him about his dad, I watch him smile to himself, looking off into the distance, like he knows one of the best secrets in the world.

GOING HOME

Kanani L. Kauka

I had come back to Hawaii because I didn't know where
else to go. It was where I'd been born and mostly raised, and
it was as close to having a home as I'd ever have. I knew I
could stay with my oldest friend, Carol. She had been urging
me to visit ever since she had inherited her aunt's house some
years earlier. I had enough money to keep me afloat for a
month. Everything, finally, seemed to be falling into place.

Carol's aunt's was an old house, settled deep in the
Manoa Valley, above the University of Hawaii campus. The
separate apartment I was to use was in the basement of the
house. It was tiny and the front had no windows at all, but
the back opened into the green, sloping garden behind the
house. My first afternoon there, Carol and I sat on the lanai
in the fading, golden light, breathing the smell of the
plumeria. There is very little twilight in Hawaii, and soon
after the sun set we were enveloped in a smooth darkness. I
told her why I was in Hawaii, all about my break-up with
Joanna and my need for some quiet time and space to think.
Carol sympathized with me, laughed in all the right places,
and assured me that I could stay as long as I needed. When
she went upstairs it was late and I was tired but relaxed,
comforted that I no longer felt as alone as I had.

I woke that night in that sudden strange way—one
moment you are asleep, the next fully awake. The house was

quiet; I could hear the rustle of fruit rats in the mango tree just outside the bedroom, but there were no other sounds. I could feel the presence of someone in the room, urging me with a look to wake up. The moonlight came through the window in patches; a breeze stirred the curtains. I could hear my own heartbeat as I slowly turned my head and looked around the room. There was no one there. I sat up and without turning on the light made my way into the living room; I could hear whispering now, a bare suggestion of voices, and the air shimmered with curiosity. The light from the stereo glowed in the darkness, although I did not think I had left it on. Feeling strangely calm, I turned the stereo off and went back to bed. I fell asleep instantly.

The next morning, Carol came down to join me for coffee. She was cheerful and friendly, asking me how I had slept. "Fine," I said, and then added abruptly, "You didn't tell me you had spirits here."

She blushed. "Did they wake you?"

I nodded. "They seemed to be wondering who I was," I said.

"I'm sorry," she said lamely. "I'm glad you weren't scared. I wasn't quite sure how to tell you. I mean, some people flip if they think they're sleeping in a haunted house. My aunt told me about them, but she said they'd never given her any trouble, and I never have any trouble, so . . ."

I smiled. "It's okay. I've been kind of wanting to get back to my roots—I guess this is as good a way as any, right?"

She looked relieved that I wasn't angry or afraid. She seemed reassured by the fact that I was clearly unfazed, and so proceeded to tell me scary stories until my hair practically stood on end. When she got to the one where her grandmother had seen a bodiless head floating outside her window one night, I made her stop. I took small comfort in the fact that all her stories were secondhand, things that had happened to other people, in places other than this house.

♦

Hawaii was the only place I could come to and be whole. My relationship with Joanna had been foundering for months, but what prompted my flight was her telling me about a course she was going to take in how to be a kahuna, a Hawaiian priest. She wasn't the only white lover I'd had who had been fascinated by my exotic ethnic background and comforted by my otherwise unremarkable middle-classness, but I grew increasingly uncomfortable as she began to ask more and more questions about all things Hawaiian. "Whose spiritual roots are you looking for?" I'd yelled during one of our many fights. She accused me of being ignorant of my own culture, and worse, of not even being interested. I began to feel a sad, ancient throb in me. The sullen Hawaiian I became only seemed to urge her on in her quest for an identity, and she seemed determined to take on mine.

Being with Carol was a relief. She, too, was *haole*, or white, but her family had been in Hawaii since the 1880s. I knew she would understand why I was there, even if I didn't quite understand yet myself. I wouldn't have to explain every detail of my life as an Exotic Hawaiian to her.

Over the next few days I made a conscious effort to reconnect with my original home. I went to the Bishop Museum, which is dedicated to the preservation and continuation of native Hawaiian culture. I did all kinds of tourist things by myself, as if I had never been there before. I went on a sunset cruise through Honolulu Harbor, and for the first time I saw the Honolulu skyline from the ocean. I went to the Polynesian Cultural Center and watched a man dressed in kapa loincloth split a coconut on a sharp stake embedded in the sand. I even went to the Big Island to see the City of Refuge, where I stood in awe beneath the palms, gazing at the grass huts and enormous, fierce statues of the gods of my ancient world, contemplating a society that could set aside holy spaces for sanctuary. If a criminal reached one, no matter what the crime, he could not be touched so long as he remained within its confines. He could fish and plant taro, and so eke out an existence, but he could not leave. Even hundreds of years later, a sense of loneliness pervaded the place.

My favorite place to go was the Pali, a tourist site on the island of Oahu. It's the lookout point nestled at the top of an enormous cliff, or *pali* in Hawaiian. The view is spectacular and dramatic, with a rolling valley and a glinting blue Pacific ocean glimmering at its base. The drop is vertiginous. Every year a couple of tourists fall off, not because they got dizzy peering over the edge, but because they gave in to the temptation to climb over the guard rail and lean into the hard steady wind that rushes across the valley and up and over the top of the pali; too late they discover that the wind is not so steady after all. And every year some ambitious rock climber is taught a very hard lesson. No one has ever made it to the top, and I've been told that technically it's not a very hard climb, but each time someone tries it, something happens to prevent the ascent. Legend has it that the bones of a king are hidden in a cave somewhere on the face of the cliff, and the sacredness of the site makes it off-limits to even the most ignorant. But what most of the tourists never realize is that this isn't just a lookout, it's also a war memorial. At the foot of the cliff lie the skeletons of hundreds of Oahu warriors. Rather than surrender to King Kamehameha, who was waging a campaign to unite the islands for the first time, the warriors flung themselves from the pali, leaving only an echo of their defiant cries on the gusts of the wind that rushes up from their collective grave.

I also went to the beach every morning, washing residual tension from my skin with salt water and sunlight. I spent a lot of time thinking about my grandmother and the stories she had told me about her girlhood on the Big Island. Sometimes she had lulled me to sleep with fantastic stories of the creation of the islands and the myths about the Hawaiian gods and goddesses, and sometimes she'd chilled my blood with ghost stories. My dreams afterward were always intense and technicolored, bright with the images of the swirling fire-goddess or the terrifying shark-god. As I lay on the beach, hearing the echo of my grandmother's voice in my head, I thought that I could die happy in Hawaii. I knew she would laugh at that. She would remind me that nothing ever really dies here. In the Hawaiian afterlife we go on as if we were alive, eating, drinking, playing games, quarreling. The islands are crowded with generations of ghosts carrying on as they did in life, running the full spectrum from those who died before the whalers and missionaries came and so spend eternity wading through taro patches and nightfishing by the light of kukui nut torches, to the Hawaiian man who died yesterday of a heart attack and so will spend his afterlife driving a bread truck and drinking Primo beer in front of the television. All of this sounded much more sensible to me than the alternative of floating around in a city paved with gold, playing a harp.

◆

I began to pick up the superstitions I'd had as a child, ones I'd discarded when I'd gone to college. I caught myself whistling one evening as I did the dishes, and I stopped abruptly when I remembered that whistling after dark attracts spirits. The ghosts in the house pretty much left me alone after that first night, although every morning I still found appliances on, as if they had been listening to music or making coffee. In the evenings when I was alone I was always aware of another presence, and sometimes it felt as if someone were brushing against me or sitting next to me on the couch. Although I was not frightened by the spirits, there were lots of old Hawaiian stories about spirits that were not so benevolent. I tried not to think about those.

I also thought about Joanna. I wondered what she would think if she knew I was living in a haunted house—though I thought of it as inhabited, not haunted—and if she would somehow approve of me more now that I was really living like a *true* Hawaiian, surrounded by the mysteries of my culture, in touch with some internal spirituality. I wondered if I could persuade her to come and stay in the apartment for a while, instead of taking the kahuna course. It made me laugh to think about it. Between me and whoever else was in this place, corporeal or not, I didn't think there was room for her. I didn't regret the abruptness of my departure from her, but I was starting to realize that we had a lot of unfinished business, or at least I did. I began to hope, so secretly that I was hardly aware of it, that she would call me when she got to Oahu; maybe here, on my turf, we could figure out what happened between us, and one way or another move on.

Now that I could imagine seeing Joanna again, I found that rather than wanting to protect Hawaii from her, I wanted to show it to her. I wanted her to see it as I did, not as the home of some spiritual salvation and mythic "roots," but as a place as ordinary and complex as any other. I could show her its stunning beauty. I constructed elaborate fantasies in which we traveled all over the state, with me as tour-guide and resident expert. Over the course of this venture she would stop obsessing over my roots and search out her own, and we would become much better friends than we had been lovers.

The day before I knew she was to leave for Hawaii I broke down and called. I left a hurried message on her answering machine, to the point: "If you have time when you get here, call me." I left my number and the address.

That night I slept badly. My dreams were chaotic, roaring, full of mythic characters and unidentifiable forms speaking an incomprehensible language. I woke twice soaked in sweat, my heart hammering, feeling none of the benevolence I had associated with the house spirits. The house was quiet, but it did not feel peaceful, and I thought I heard voices in the ravine below the garden. The night was cloudy and dark, the rustling in the mango tree outside was suddenly menacing. After lying there for a while, I finally got up, exasperated with myself, but unable to quell my nervousness. I made tea and turned on all the lights in apartment. Upstairs, I heard the floorboards creak. Carol—I hoped it was Carol—was moving around. A few minutes later she knocked at my door.

She was pale. "Did you hear it?"

"I thought I heard voices," I said cautiously. "In the ravine, down below."

She nodded and accepted a cup of tea from me. "This isn't the first time I've heard them," she said between sips, trembling a little. "But they've never been so loud before."

I tried to lighten the mood. "It's probably just the Nightmarchers," I joked, realizing as soon as the words were out of my mouth that it might not be so funny.

She curled into an armchair. "Tell me," she whispered.

I drew the curtains tighter. I wasn't so sure this was the time for ghost stories, especially since I had my doubts about the supposed nonexistence of these beings. My grandmother had frightened the daylights out of me with some of her stories, and I wasn't sure I wanted the honor of passing them on. Carol looked at me expectantly.

"Well," I began, "according to my grandmother, who is a proper Hawaiian lady who is Mormon and was raised on the Big Island, and who has a healthy respect for all things spiritual, the Nightmarchers are groups of warriors and a member or members of the *ali'i*, the royalty."

"You mean their spirits, right?" Carol interjected.

"Yeah. I mean, they're doing just what they did in life, escorting the king or queen or whoever to wherever they were going. And they're still doing it, and all the *kapus*, the taboos, are still in place. So this is what happens, according to my grandmother, if you meet the Nightmarchers some night: you will hear them before you see them, and you should try to get out of their path. If it's too late to get out of the way, then you have to take off all your clothes"

Here Carol raised an eyebrow, and I laughed. "I know, I know, whatever. But that's what you're supposed to do: strip naked and then lie face down on the ground, and whatever you do when they pass, don't look up. If you look upon the king or queen, you are put to death. Also, if they feel like it, they can put you to death even if you haven't broken a kapu. But if you're lucky enough to have an ancestor among the marchers, you can be spared. So that's what you should do if you ever meet the Nightmarchers."

I sat back, relieved that in the retelling, the tale did not seem so frightening. Carol was less pale. "I've never heard some of the stories you've told me," she said, her voice low. "I've lived here all my life, and I never knew any of this."

I shrugged. "You didn't grow up in a native Hawaiian family with a grandmother who's seen it all." I said. "You must know some of it. I mean, you live in a house inhabited by spirits."

"I know." She shook her head slowly and sipped her tea. "But I never thought very much about it, until you came back and started telling me these stories. And to be honest, I didn't really believe my aunt about the ghosts. I hardly ever heard anything, really, until you came."

I felt a ripple up my spine. I thought of the terror I had felt when my grandmother told me about the Nightmarchers—I had seen it through her eyes. She had grown up in extreme isolation in the Waipio Valley on the Big Island, and had often seen the spirits of those long dead fishing at night in the bay; she had heard the click of the smooth stones used to play games and gamble, although no players could be seen. Through her, I had looked into a world that was simultaneously long gone and present all around us. Now Carol was seeing this world through me. I stood and pulled the curtains back. The sky had gone from dark gray to a strange pink. It was day.

Carol went back to bed. I stayed up, drinking coffee and thinking. I woke several hours later, stiff from having fallen asleep on the too-short couch. The phone was ringing.

♦

"Hello?" I said, my mouth gluey with sleep.

"Hey," said a familiar voice. "It's me."

I sat down. "Joanna?"

She had come a few days before her course started; I'd be able to fulfill my tour-guide fantasy. Joanna was attentive and respectful, asked intelligent questions. She was affectionate and funny. I was confused. I had spent the past several weeks working up a healthy sense of detachment for Joanna. I knew I didn't love her anymore, but I felt an enormous, unsettling pride in showing her everything I loved most in the world. I showed her where I'd gone to school, where I'd lived, took her on a cruise of Honolulu Harbor at sunset. I made the Night of the Nightmarchers, as Carol and I had taken to calling it, into a funny story. When I took her to the Pali she swayed gently against the guard rail as I told her about the Oahu warriors throwing themselves to their deaths, her eyes fixed on the view. She did not laugh at my Night of the Nightmarchers story. She did not ask for details about the "strange occurrences" I alluded to. I almost began to believe that she had given up her notion of becoming a kahuna and was here only out of polite interest and a desire not to forfeit the money she had paid for the class.

Her last night in Honolulu I offered to cook dinner for her. I wanted us to have one evening when there were no distractions, no excuses for not talking about the things we had been carefully stepping around for days now. I was very

tired; I had not slept well for three nights running. All the
sounds in the house seemed to be magnified, and each night I
was jerked out of sleep by the sudden rising murmur of
voices, as if a great crowd were in the garden. On the second
night, I realized that they were speaking Hawaiian. I even
got up to look out the window to see for myself; the
murmuring force of the invisible crowd was so great that I
almost believed that I could see something. This went on
until dawn, when the sounds gradually became a whisper
and then died out all together at sunrise. I never sensed any
menace or hostility. It was as if I didn't exist for them at all. I
hadn't told Joanna about any of this. This was something
that, after all my tour-guiding, I wanted to keep solely for
myself. I knew Carol had heard them too, for she was
looking as raccoon-eyed as I was. On my way to pick Joanna
up at her hotel, I impulsively knocked on Carol's door.

"The Night of the Nightmarchers you said something
odd," I said. "You said you never heard any of this stuff
until I came."

Carol tilted her head a little. "Well," she said slowly, "I
didn't mean that, exactly. I have heard things, felt things. But
maybe once a year, not every night, a few times a night. My
microwave never went on by itself before."

I burst out laughing. "They do that to you too?" I
gasped. "They listen to music and drink coffee at my place."

She smiled and shook her head. "Must be your
overpowering charisma," she teased, but her smile dimmed.
"It is weird, though, you know? That all of this stuff is
happening." She turned to go back inside. "Maybe they're
just glad you're home."

I left to pick up Joanna feeling calmer than I had in days.
The house was dark when Joanna and I got back; Carol
must have gone out. Throughout the evening the house
behaved normally. Nothing went on or off by itself; the
sounds in the garden were the ordinary whispers of wind
and night animals. I found I couldn't ask any of the
questions I wanted. I couldn't decide if we were moving
toward some inevitable confrontation or if our split was so
profound that there was no point in talking about it, that we
were speaking different languages. Her desire to take what I
viewed as mine—my history, my culture—which had struck

me as so supremely arrogant a few months before now seemed almost irrelevant. She would take her class and feel like a kahuna, or something, and then go back home, tell everybody what she'd done, and in three years have forgotten all about it. No harm came to Hawaii. Long after all the seekers had gone, the islands would still be crowded with ghosts. She had not heard or seen or sensed any of the power at the Pali or even here in this house. She had read the history books, listened to the music, gained a greater appreciation for a culture other than her own. What she had missed was the living element of it. She was utterly unaware of the magic that surrounded her. She could learn the chants and dances, the cosmology of Hawaiian beliefs, but she would never see the Nightmarchers, never hear the voices of the dead, never feel their presence. She would never see beyond the surface. Carol, although she was also *haole*, had a real connection with Hawaii. She loved it and respected it like I did. We shared the Night of the Nightmarchers; Joanna never could.

After I drove Joanna back to her hotel, I made a detour on the way home and went to the Pali. I leaned against the guard rail, feeling that deceptive wind push against me, seducing me. The night glittered with stars and the lights of a few houses and cars. I stood dreaming with my eyes open, seeing young Hawaiians throwing themselves triumphantly from the cliff, going to their deaths certain that they had escaped tyranny. Did they relive that moment forever in the afterlife? I saw them fall and disappear into the treetops below. I heard their voices call out to their gods and one another. I would return to an inhabited house and fall asleep to the murmurs and whispers of my ancestors.

CONTRIBUTORS

BARBARA WILSON is the author of five mystery novels, including *Gaudi Afternoon*, which first introduced Cassandra Reilly and which received a British Crime Writers Award for best mystery set in Europe and a Lambda Literary Award for Best Lesbian Mystery. Her most recent mystery is *Trouble in Transylvania*.

ELLEN S. KORR is currently at work on *The Outsider*, a lesbian romance novel set in Pennsylvania's Lancaster County. Ellen resides in West Chester, Pennsylvania with her life partner of twelve years.

G.V. BABISH lives outside Philadelphia, where she is a part-time teacher of personal computer software and a part-time writer of scary neighbor stories. G.V. lives with one cat, Sally Taylforth, who helps her with part-time activities.

J.D. SHAW was born and raised in Michigan, and has lived in many U.S. cities, including New Orleans and Boston. She now lives near Philadelphia. She is married and has three grown daughters, all living in Boston. She recently completed *Provenance of a Murder*, a novel featuring Harry Hutchinson, and is working on a book of short stories featuring this same detective.

JEWELLE GOMEZ is the author of the double Lambda Literary Award-winning Black lesbian vampire novel *The Gilda*

Stories and *Forty-Three Septembers*, a book of essays. After living in New York for 22 years, Jewelle now resides in San Francisco.

JOANNE DAHME is a life-long resident of Philadelphia and the surrounding suburbs. She holds a bachelor's degree in civil engineering from Villanova University and a master's degree in journalism from Temple University. Joanne works for the Public Affairs Division of the Philadelphia Water Department and presently lives in Philadelphia's Roxborough district with her husband and son. She is the author of two novels.

KANANI L. KAUKA is the assistant editor of *Lambda Book Report*. She grew up in Hawaii and Boston, Massachusetts. She lives in Takoma Park, Maryland, with her lover and three cats.

KATHERINE V. FORREST is the author of several novels that feature detective Kate Delafield: *Amateur City*, *Murder at the Nightwood Bar* (now a feature film, *Nightwood Bar*, with Mary Louise Parker and Tom Arnold), and the Lambda Literary Award winners *The Beverly Malibu* and *Murder By Tradition*. Born in Canada and a long-time resident of Los Angeles, Katherine now lives in San Francisco. Her most recent novel is the political thriller *Flashpoint*.

KATHLEEN DOWNEY is a New York State native who has also lived in Boston and Los Angeles. She now resides in the Philadelphia area with her two cocker spaniels. She is the author of *Murder in the New Age*, a mystery.

LINDA K. WRIGHT is an officer of the Meridian Writers' Cooperative and is the award-winning author of numerous poems and short stories. Her work has appeared in several anthologies, including *Thirteen by Seven*. She currently lives in Malvern, Pennsylvania with her husband.

LISA D. WILLIAMSON enjoys scuba diving and racquet sports when not in front of her computer. She currently lives in the Philadelphia suburbs with her husband and two sons, and has just completed her first mystery novel.

MABEL MANEY is an artist and the author of the Nancy Clue mysteries *The Case of the Not-So-Nice Nurse* and *The Case of the Good-For-Nothing Girlfriend*. She lives happily in San Francisco with Miss Lily Bee.

MEREDITH SUZANNE BAIRD is the author of *Romancing the Romaine—Adventures of Valentine Willowthigh*, a satire on romance fiction. She received First Prize in Short Non-Fiction from the 1992 Philadelphia Writers' Conference and First Prizes in Mystery Novel Writing, Short Fiction, and Short Non-Fiction from the 1993 Philadelphia Writers' Conference. A 22-year resident of Southern California, Meredith now lives in Malvern, Pennsylvania with her husband and eight cats.

NIKKI BAKER is the author of the mysteries *In the Game*, *The Lavender House Murder*, and *Long Goodbyes*, all of which feature African-American sleuth Virginia Kelly. A life-long Midwesterner and a former resident of Chicago, Nikki currently lives in the San Francisco Bay area.

RUTHANN ROBSON is the author of two collections of short fiction, *Eye of a Hurricane* (1989), for which she won both a Lambda Literary Award and the Ferro-Grumley Award, and *Cecile* (1991). She is also the author of *Lesbian (Out)Law: Survival Under the Rule of Law*, as well as numerous articles in law reviews, periodicals, and anthologies that seek to develop a lesbian legal theory. Her newest work is *Another Mother*, a novel about a lesbian attorney who defends lesbian mothers. Robson lives in New York, where she is a professor of law at the City University of New York (CUNY) Law School.

TEE A. CORINNE was born in Florida in 1943, moved North for graduate school in 1966 and West to San Francisco for the gay seventies. Since 1981 she has lived, written, and made art in the woods of Southern Oregon. Her books include *The Cunt Coloring Book, Yantras of Womanlove, Dreams of the Woman Who Loved Sex, Lovers, The Sparkling Lavender Dust of Lust*, and *Courting Pleasure*. She is the art books columnist for *Feminist Bookstore News*, a founding board member and founding co-chair of the Lesbian/Gay Caucus (an affiliated society of the College Art Association), and a national board member of the Women's Caucus for Art.

VICTORIA A. BROWNWORTH is a syndicated columnist for the *Philadelphia Daily News*. Her work appears in numerous queer and mainstream publications, including *The Advocate*, *The Village Voice*, *Spin*, and *Out*. She is the author of six books and currently lives in Philadelphia with her partner, filmmaker Judith M. Redding, six cats, and one dog.

Other Mysteries from Third Side Press

Timber City Masks by Kieran York. Introducing Royce Madison, sheriff's department diehard deputy and softspoken dyke-about-town. Royce explores the boundaries of sexuality, racial prejudice, family loyalty, and small-town fear as she searches for the murderer of her lover's best friend.

> *"An entertaining read . . . filled with rich descriptions and colorful characters."* —*Small Press*
>
> *"I enjoy Kieran York's work, and I can't wait to read more of it."* —*Sandra Scoppettone*

$9.95   1-879427-13-3

Crystal Mountain Veils by Kieran York. As if finding out who killed tabloid gossip monger Sandra Holt weren't challenge enough, Timber County's acting sheriff Royce Madison also has to deal with a drifter stalking her girlfriend and an election opponent who's ready to fight dirty. With the Family Morals Coalition pumping big bucks into her opponent's campaign and everybody in town anxious for her to make an arrest, Royce has to dig deep. $10.95   1-879427-19-2

To order any Third Side Press book or to receive a free catalog, write to Third Side Press, 2250 W. Farragut, Chicago, IL 60625-1802. When ordering books, please include $2 shipping for the first book and .50 for each additional book.

Third Side Press
because every issue has more than two sides.

The book you are holding is the product of work by an independent women's book publishing company.